DEAN'S WAY OUT

Copyright © 2020 by Dean Lin

The right of Dean Lin to be identified as the Author has been asserted in accordance with the Copyright, Design and Patents Act of 1988.

All rights reserved. No part of this publication may be reproduced, distributed, or transmitted in any form or by any means, including photocopying, recording, or other electronic or mechanical methods, without the prior written permission of the publisher or the author. This book may not be lent, resold, hired out or otherwise disposed of by way of trade in any form other than in which it is published without the prior written consent from the author and publisher.

Although the publisher and the author have made every effort to ensure that the information in this book was correct at press time and while this publication is designed to provide accurate information in regard to the subject matter covered, the publisher and the author assume no responsibility for errors, inaccuracies, omissions, or any other inconsistencies herein and hereby disclaim any liability to any party for any loss, damage, or disruption caused by errors or omissions, whether such errors or omissions result from negligence, accident, or any other cause.

This publication is meant as a source of valuable information for the reader, however it is not meant as a substitute for direct expert assistance. If such level of assistance is required, the services of a competent professional should be sought.

Published in the United States by Live Your Dreams Out Loud Publishing
Cover Photo by Lexa Payne

ISBN: 978-0-578-65962-6 (Paperback)

Printed in the United States of America

First Edition

www.deanwlin.com
dean@deanwlin.com

DEAN'S WAY OUT

How Overcoming Eating Disorders, Trauma, and Depression Made Me Fabulous!

Dean Lin

A *Live Your Dreams Out Loud* Publishing

LOS ANGELES | NEW YORK

For anyone who's ever felt pain, sadness, and loneliness—I hope you know how loved you are.

I dedicate this book to friends that have become family and to my sister, Cindy. I also dedicate this to you. I love you all so much and I am grateful every single day to have your support.

GLITTER A.F. CONTENTS

DYING

FOREWORD	9
CHAPTER 1 | DYING TO BE PERFECT	15
CHAPTER 2 | A RAINBOW WAS BORN	19
CHAPTER 3 | NOT-SO GOLDEN CHILD	23
CHAPTER 4 | DYING TO FIT IN	31
CHAPTER 5 | DEAN VS. DICKS	37
CHAPTER 6 | HIGH SCHOOL (NOT) MUSICAL	45
CHAPTER 7 | O.M.G. YOU'RE AN INSPIRATION	53
CHAPTER 8 | I ~~AM ASIAN~~ WANTED TO BE WHITE	57
CHAPTER 9 | BYE, QUEENS!	65

HEALING

CHAPTER 10 | THERAPY, WHO IS SHE?	73
CHAPTER 11 | LOSING MY REHAB VIRGINITY	79
CHAPTER 12 | LORD… AGAIN? A-FUCKING-GAIN?	85
CHAPTER 13 | I'M BACK, BITCHES!	89
CHAPTER 14 | THIRD TIME'S A CHARM	95
CHAPTER 15 | MAY 10TH, 2016	99
CHAPTER 16 | DEAN VS. ED	103
CHAPTER 17 | NOURISHING THE FABULOUS TRAUMA	113
CHAPTER 18 | THAT SHIT AIN'T WORTH IT	117

LIVING

CHAPTER 19 | FUCK DREAMS (THAT AREN'T YOUR DREAMS)	125
CHAPTER 20 | REJECTIONS ARE THE BEST	129
CHAPTER 21 | STRUT, STEP, AND GLITTER	137
CHAPTER 22 | GOING FOR IT (AND BEING FABULOUS ALL THE WAY)	141
CHAPTER 23 | NOT FOR FAME, NOT FOR CLOUT	147
CHAPTER 24 | A LOVE LETTER TO YOU	153
ACKNOWLEDGMENTS	157

FOREWORD

Brian D. Johnson

Wait a minute, did I get asked to write the Foreword to Dean's Way Out? No way, Dean! This is unbelievable! Why would I start a foreword off in such a manner questioning this honor? Well, this is like an official baptizing and deliverance for me.

I was born and raised in the bible belt and was homophobic growing up. I was conditioned to be ignorant and programmed to not question my ignorance. I never did. I just thought that it was wrong and never cared to ask WHY. The idea of being gay growing up wasn't the norm, nor was it accepted in my environment–programming and conditioning my ignorance.

It wasn't until I got a chance to get out of my environment, that I was able to reflect on my ignorance. Looking back at the ignorance I had growing up in terms of being homophobic, I understand that my homophobia was the same as the racism that I have experienced my entire life.

I can't imagine the number of people who have felt trapped, victimized, and had to deal with it throughout the existence of humanity. My homophobic position changed for me back in 2008. My mentor, who I never thought was gay, told me that he was a gay man and had once struggled to come out. I was in total shock and concerned.

As time went on, he provided me with insight and perspective that changed my life. He educated me on my ignorance. It was the first time I got an insight into what it was like for someone who had been trapped to not know if they had any "way out."

If you haven't learned anything from my ignorance, or if you have your own pinned up discrimination, please, ask yourself WHY. Furthermore, if you haven't traveled and been exposed to other human beings, it's a must, you aren't the only human in the world. The world is beautiful and made up of 7 billion people who are different.

Dean's Way Out is the antithesis to my adolescence. A young kid born in Queens whose parents are immigrants from China came to America as **DREAMERS**. Dean experienced discrimination his entire life and is now on a mission to maximize his human existence and inspire the world.

When I was first asked to write this Foreword, I was honored but challenged on my approach. How honest do I want to be? Well, that's the point, right?

I first met Dean while working on the Emmy award-winning show, Carpool Karaoke. Dean, a polarizing individual on appearance, has an aura about him that commands greatness—a blonde Mohawk, stonewashed jeans, with a t-shirt tucked in, white shoes, and a pace that's faster than the NYC strut.

As I've gotten to know Dean, I've realized that he has so much to offer. He's on a mission to inspire the world. More importantly, he continues to do the work on himself. He's turned his trauma and pain into a masterful story.

I know that this book is needed on so many levels for the world. You made a decision to commit and share your story with the world. Thank You! The three phases of this book are straight forward, honest, and will speak to anybody.

Thank you, Dean, for allowing me to write this Foreword and be a part of your journey. Your presence and soul uplifts me daily, and I'm glad that you are Buddha and Buddha is you.

DYING

CHAPTER ONE

Dying to Be Perfect

Since the day I was born, I believed I was unlovable, worthless, unattractive and that people in my life would hurt me. Wait—let's not get ahead of ourselves. Besides, maybe I'm being dramatic, because when am I not? I was destined to be a drama queen that no one expected to enter their lives, including you.

Queens, my life is perfect now that I'm about to tell you the tea of my life. Okay, no, just kidding. I wish that were the case, but it's really not. Truth is, having destructive behaviors and having parents molding you into a self-hating gay really changes the path life takes you. Sounds cliché, I know, bitch. Just settle down, and I'll get to the story.

May 10th, 2016: it was the worst and best day of my life. My sister, Cindy, was texting me non-stop as I was cleaning my dorm room and getting ready to enter rehab for the third time. We texted back and forth about old conversations—times when my life was a mess and I had been debating if I should go to treatment or keep using destructive behaviors until my deathbed. I was a ball of anxiety because I wanted to flee. But for anyone who can relate, anxiety always helps me clean. And girl, I needed to clean that dorm room because I could not afford to be in more debt.

We're throwing it back to the end of my first year in college. I was in a fraternity and my "brothers" were nice enough to offer to drive me to Thousand Oaks, where my treatment center was.

"Well, are you ready?"

At that moment, I still felt like the world was against me, but I pretended I was fine. I didn't need their pity. I didn't need anyone's pity. I didn't want to go to treatment anyway, until my sister called me before I walked out of my empty dorm room.

Do you know how awkward it was for me? Puh-lease. I know you prefer texting over phone calls any day. I LOVED texting because it meant I didn't really have to show my emotions, which was a skill I had mastered. It was random that we ended up on the phone together, but I am so glad that we did. There was a lot of silence. Not much back and forth until it got closer and closer to the time I had to leave.

It was nice to hear my sister's voice. It was a voice three thousand miles away but still felt close to my heart. Okay, that sounds very "in my feelings," but you get what I mean.

"Are you ready?" Her voice cracked.

Quite honestly, I didn't know if I was ready. I didn't know if I was capable of giving up years of destructive behaviors in exchange for health. I know it sounds crazy. I was lost for words, even to a simple question like that. I was broken.

"Please don't tell Mom and Dad. I need to do this." I was desperate to run away from my issues and desperate to heal at the same time.

This war inside me had gone on for so long, longer than I knew I was gay. And hun, that is a LONG time. My sister must have a sixth sense. She knew to be mean to me 90% of the time, but somehow, she won me over 10% of the time. She was the most nurturing person I knew.

"I know, okay?"

"It's just, they've caused me so much pain, and I don't know if I can heal with them anywhere near me or knowing my whereabouts."

"I just need you to take care of yourself, okay? I didn't know most of my life that you struggled with things like this, and I feel like a shitty sister for not being there for you."

She started crying, so I started crying. My heart broke into a million pieces. How did she know exactly what to say? I felt years of pent-up emotions come out and my chest felt heavy, even if I was a pile of bones. My back slid down the door. I sat there crying. I remember holding my chest like I could not breathe. This was the moment I knew.

I had spent so many years stripping away my identity and restricting not only food but also everything else in my life. I let my eating disorder consume me. I thought destructive habits would help me overcome the negative thoughts, but they became louder. I turned to food for comfort and control because I couldn't control my sexuality, my identity, and how others treated me.

Negative self-talk gave me the illusion of being in control, but in reality, I was out of control. Bulimia and anorexia helped me cope with these feelings of not being good enough.

Till this day, my sister texts me from time to time and says that moment "fucked her up."

Is there someone in your life, dead or alive, who helped you through an extremely dark time? Who are they, and what significance did they bring into your life?

CHAPTER TWO

A Rainbow Was Born

Okay, let's back it up a bit. I wanted to give you a free preview, minus the advertisements. If you're like me, you make up fantasy entrances to liven up the story. I'm extra, I know. You'll know too. Give me a few more sentences.

At 6:33 AM, November 30th, 1997, a rainbow was born out of Satan. I need to relax. I'm kidding, sorry Mom. A slightly LESS rainbow baby was born because I was rushed into the emergency room immediately after labor. The Lord was literally testing me. Even before I was born, my mom got into a slight car accident with me in her belly! I'm totally not exaggerating on this one. Y'all really didn't want me here, huh? Ugh, homophobia. HAHA, just kidding.

ANYWAYS, I always think back to that story she told me. Every time she told it, I was so mad she didn't sue the guy! Maybe we could have been as rich as the Kardashians, you know? Girl, I could have been fabulous AND a self-made billionaire. Maybe then being in the closet would have paid off.

Growing up, I didn't really know who my parents were until I was about four and a half years old. I remember living in China with my aunt, my grandma, and my cousin. My family was from a smaller town in China called Fujian.

So, for the first four and a half years of my life, that's what I knew but looking back, I think what affected me the most was the fact that my parents threw me away—okay, they didn't really throw me away, but you get what I mean.

They gave me away when I was a few months old, so that was a type of separation anxiety that my therapist said I must have faced as a kid, being separated from the only thing I knew, which probably caused my trust issues to rise. Tea.

I don't really remember much from the four and a half years I was in China except distinct moments. I just remember growing up speaking Chinese, so that's probably why I still know some Chinese to this day. I also remember being scared of my cousin, because every time I took her toys, she would smack me or scold me. I am probably exaggerating right now—she probably just lightly tapped my hand. See, I think I was really born as a drama queen and was destined to be dramatic. I seem to blow up my memories; perhaps its from suppressed trauma?

Well, to be fair, they were the ones who raised me and formed me into the person I am today, so I'm grateful for that, but I don't remember or recall if they ever let me talk to my parents back in the United States when I was in China.

When you're at that age you don't really remember phone calls, and there wasn't FaceTime during those years, which was like 1997 to 2002. The times I remember there were honestly some of my better memories because that was when I kind of had forgotten the separation anxiety.

Take school, for an example. I remember having fun; I

had that playful relationship you have in a good attachment to certain family members. I was such a goofball, and I would pretend that I was sick and that my stomach hurt. But the second my aunt told me I didn't need to go back to school, I was like, "Oh my God, I feel so much better! Let's go get McDonald's or something." HAHA, I was the devil's child.

I remember my life starting to change when I was four and a half. I flew from China to the United States with my grandma on my mom's side. All I remember was running to the airport doors crying for my aunt and my other grandma on my dad's side; they were the two women who raised me up to that point.

I am so grateful I had such strong women who raised me the years my parents could not, but that doesn't erase the negative effect it had on me mentally; I felt like I must have been so unlovable to have been given up by my parents at such a young age.

My parents tried to rationalize their decision throughout my childhood, telling me they had to make ends meet and get money when they immigrated from China. They were in a huge amount of debt, and they had to work really long hours. Girl, maybe I would have trusted them if I hadn't seen all the fucking family vacations they had gone on without me! To this day, I don't have those family pictures my parents and my sister have. This is most likely the reason why her life turned out more mentally stable. Tea spilled.

So at this point, I was four and a half, and I had already gone through two types of "separation anxieties," which in psychology is called a hierarchy of needs, But girl, what do I know? I have never been a good student.

With my needs not being met, I learned to use food to numb my emotions. This started when I tried to escape my parents' arms at the airport in the winter of 2002. Just imagine little Dean with a little ponytail on the back of his neck, being scared out of his mind and getting into a car with complete strangers. My parents lived in Queens, New York, so I call it home. I remember when I first got to my new "home," my dad fed me this crab soup. Girl, I remember eating all of it until I could not move because I was feeling such intense emotion, and this was one of the moments that led the foundation to my future struggles. It's crazy how I learned to numb my emotions using food. I started developing a binge eating disorder at just four and a half years old, which started the domino effect that led to more destructive behaviors later on in my life.

CHAPTER THREE

Not-So Golden Child

Hun, you're probably wondering why I'm telling you this story and some parts of my childhood that I don't remember, What I can say is that these were the moments stemmed my trust issues (I learned this later in life, during therapy). I always felt fear around my mom and dad because I was constantly worrying if I was going to get hit by them.

I was a playful kid and I didn't know how to, quote on quote, "behave" or conform to society's expectations of what it means to be a boy. I had ADHD and was only recently prescribed medications to help with that, because mental health does not exist in traditional Asian households. Give me a shout if you can relate, girl.

So, with all this energy I had and this ball of fabulousness that now I can see myself as, I used school as a way to act out to gain my parents' approval and attention. I just felt like I was the sibling who no one really cared about, so my only friend was food. Whenever I was afraid of doing something wrong, or if I did do something wrong and wanted to cry, my parents would yell at me, telling me that I should man-up and suppress my emotions because it wasn't like a boy to cry so much. And looking back, suppressing all my emotions was really detrimental to my life. I wanted to be so strong that nothing could shake me to a point where I was bawling my eyes out, and it took me years to regain the ability to be vulnerable and sensitive.

Every single week, or maybe even every day, I don't even remember, I would be sent home with notes from my kindergarten teacher telling my parents how naughty I was and how I had lashed out at the other kids.

But the tea is that I only lashed out and was expressing my anger in school towards other kids because I was having a troubled home life that didn't satisfy my needs of belonging; I was always an outcast in that way. I didn't know how to be in a home where I didn't feel like I could trust myself or trust my parents; this really had an effect on me.

The education system didn't help at all either, the fact that they grade students and don't really consider how home life affects performance is trash. Every single teacher I've had has given me a pit-in-my-stomach feeling, like someone was punching me every single time I entered class because I was so scared of messing up and getting in trouble. Every time a teacher yelled at me, it would remind me of my parents yelling at me and scolding me, telling me how worthless I was and how I would be nothing in this world.

Second grade was one of the years I will never forget. In second grade, my fear of my mom increased even more and made me wish I hadn't been born. My mom forced me to memorize my multiplication tables in the second grade. I was so young and didn't have the mental capacity, and I had ADHD, which my mom probably didn't even know or consider. So, I was unable to memorize my multiplication tables because I had all this mental baggage and issues I was holding onto. But of course, the girl did not understand. So, she hit and abused me.

Why do Asian parents, or strict parents in general, think hitting their kid is okay? That just made me resent her even more. As the days went on without being able to memorize my multiplication tables, my mom decided it would be a good idea to kick my ass out of the house.

Girl, who the hell does that to a second-grade child trying to memorize multiplication tables? She literally took a bag, threw me out and left me screaming at the front door. In all other scenarios, a kid would be crying. But no, my ass gave no fucks acting like I didn't just get whooped on the booty.

I asked her, "Where's my blanket? You only gave me clothes in this bag."

What did I tell you? I am obnoxious. Oops, sorry not sorry!

Honestly, that's really my personality though. Literally the last thing someone would think of while being kicked out is a blanket. What about the fact that you're in second grade and you need food, or more importantly… WATER?!

Anyway, I remember yelling at her in my head, and this was the moment I started growing resentment, fear and hatred towards my mother.

I screamed out in the universe, "You're the worst fucking mother anyone could have ever asked for."

I wasn't sorry for it in the moment, I was really angry and sad at the same time, but I didn't know how to express my emotions. This is when I was grateful for my father, who came home and told my mom that she was being nuts. He stopped her and took me back inside. That night, I was shaking in my bed, not knowing if my mom was going to come into my room and abuse the fuck out of me. But wait, don't sympathize with Dad just yet. I mean, you can if you want, but the story gets uglier.

I repressed that night for so long. A week? A month? Years? Yeah okay, I'm getting the days and weeks mixed up. That's what happens when you suppress trauma, okay?! Don't do it!

So anyway, my petty ass snitched on my mom the next whatever day for hitting me, and the school asked her to go in, but she was afraid of getting taken away by Child Protective Services. Like Mom, what is the truth? No one told you to hit me? Eventually, she made my dad go to my school. She needed him to basically lie to the school and say that I was living under a "safe" household.

It was kind of a power trip for me. I remember the principal calling me and my sister into his office. My ass was still livid and kind of thriving off this energy. Ugh, Lord, I feel like a psycho even talking about this because my sister was crying and saying, "Oh my God, don't take my mom to jail."

My petty ass was standing there showing them a physical demonstration of the actions to mimic how my mom hit me. I looked dumb, but imagine me using my hand and slapping my butt just to show the principal I was getting spanked at home.

Only, I wish she had used her hands, but she had used hangers—METAL ones! If this was out of context, this might be a problem, but also, I was in second grade, so let's not get sexual—yet.

My dad essentially lied and "cleared things up," saying I was exaggerating, and honestly, this is one of the times in my life that I was not exaggerating, so y'all should have trusted me. Child Protective Services were on point for a quarter of a second, then I was forced to brush it off. Ugh, whatever.

My mom was livid when I got home and asked me two

questions that night that changed my perspective on her for the rest of my life. You know when people say that sticks and stones may break your bones but words will never hurt you?

WELL, they lied.

The two questions she asked me are ones I can't even fathom saying to anyone in my life, let alone my own kid that I'll have in the future.

She asked me, "Do you want me to drown you right here, or do you want to get the fuck out of the house?"

First of all, who the fuck asks their kid if they want to be drowned? This is the type of abuse that really affected me as a kid. Can you imagine believing that losing face is more important than your child's life? This is a prime example of gaslighting. I was conditioned to associate the abuse and lash-outs with acts of love from my parents. Well hun, don't trust that shit. I did, and it did not lead me down a cute path.

A family friend's daughter, basically my second cousin now, Judy, was there asking me if I was okay. I appreciate you, doll. Thank you for trying to help me out of my mother's abuse. But I'm glad we met because you literally saw me go through this trauma. To everyone around me who was an adult, my mother's behavior was considered normal, which was the insane part. Judy and I still joke about how we made it out of our childhoods alive.

Anyway, gaslighting is a way for people to feel better about themselves while taking their corrupted past and abusing you—they turn the self-love you were born with into self-hatred. I realized later in life that growing up in an unsafe household made me susceptible to unsafe situations as I grew older. Gaslighting is real.

When someone claims they love you as an excuse for the abuse they have done, it ain't love, HONEY! Thus, I was seeking out experiences and attracting the same type of energy and negativity my parents exuded on me. See, it's all learned when we are innocent kids, when we were all meant to glitter.

When you are taught that emotional manipulation and abuse equates to love, then you will not be able to seek out environments and people in your life who truly love you and care about you—unless you take steps to unlearn that.

What are examples of past relationships you've had, either romantic or friendships, that can be examples of gaslighting? What helped you overcome it? Or, what steps can you take to overcome existing manipulative relationships in your life?

CHAPTER FOUR

Dying to Fit In

If you haven't guessed already, I was a feminine kid and definitely more fabulous than the straight men who surrounded me. New York City was not as accepting as you'd think.

I mean, I get it. Y'all want to fit in too, but that doesn't mean you have to bring others down. Legends and people who made history rarely fit in, so I wasn't meant to fit in anyway. This gaysian was meant to stand out. I remember watching a show called *Totally Spies*, one of my guilty pleasures. I may or may not still watch it from time to time. If any of you know what I'm talking about, you're probably a girl or gay like me. Holla! I channeled one of the main characters, Clover, who made me feel like a bad bitch who could accomplish everything by being fabulous. So, should I credit my personality to Cartoon Network? Oop.

Every day at school, I would do the "whatever" with the

hand motions and all. If I was a teacher and saw a kid be himself, I would be snapping and clapping.

But no, no applause for me—I deserved one though!

My demeanor, my voice, and my bodily gestures were considered too girly to all the kids around me. I deviated from the norms and was punished because of it. This was before the G.B.F., or gay best friend, became an accessory for people to latch on to. The bullying wasn't as bad at school this time in my life. It was easy for me to suppress everything happening at school because I was afraid of going home.

Getting bullied at school was nothing compared to the bullying I faced at home. The constant fear of not being good enough, an outcast, and not fitting my parents' image of me followed me everywhere like a shadow. I honestly sat down one day asking if I could be like Peter Pan and lose my shadow once in a while so that I didn't have to carry all the baggage around.

I continued binge eating as a way to cope with everything happening around me. I did not want to face it head-on; if I had tried, my ass would have been crying every second of every day. There was this market next to my schools called the Unit Market. It was my safe haven. Shoutout to y'all! But also, not really. Every opportunity I got to gather the coins to afford food, I would spend them. Is that where I get my impulsiveness to spend money? Lord, I hope not. To be completely honest, I'm pretty mad chips aren't 25 cents anymore. You know those small chip bags I'm talkin' about? AND dunkaroos? AH, the only part of my childhood I miss.

Ok, that's a lie. I also miss authentic Asian food. Ya know? The food white kids made fun of? But of course, they are now proud owners of restaurant chains that benefit from Asian cuisine. Excuse me? Pause. Y'all was eating cheese sandwiches when I was eating some gourmet-ass Asian food but wanted to make me feel bad about it. But who was really winning? Ok tea, not really me because I wanted to fit in so bad. I ended up converting to peanut butter and jelly sandwiches and them nasty cookie-crust pizzas that were stale AF.

Moving on before my ADHD gets us more off track. No one really cared if I was "healthy" until my binge eating started to show physically, but to be fair, a girl didn't know better. I would always throw tantrums when my grandma wouldn't let me eat fried food, chocolate, or any type of snack. I don't blame her though; my parents kept telling her to say no to me. Sorry Grandma, but thank you for making my favorite dish every night: fried calamari.

I ate that shit up.

I think I started to realize my problems with eating a lot of food, but I still didn't really care enough to admit it. I would try to control myself and "save" some food for later or for the next day's dinner, but I couldn't. The separation anxiety I had felt from my parents as an adolescent and at four and a half years old was familiar to how I felt about food. I always thought that somehow food would grow legs and run away from me, so I had to make sure I ate it all so it wouldn't "leave" me like my parents had.

These were the last moments in my childhood that I remember where I wasn't focused on my weight. I didn't mind the way I looked but extended family, friends of my family, and my parents started to comment on my weight. My weight took up a majority of conversations I had with anyone. It's like my glitter AF personality was *invisible* to them; they only saw me as my weight.

I didn't think I needed to give a fuck about the way I looked, until I learned I had to. I was society's definition of "fat," which to my parents was the WORST thing I could be. I can vividly replay the moment when my mom starved me. She said I couldn't eat lunch and had to starve because I was "too fat." Like okay, go off and just teach your kid unhealthy behaviors. My parents obviously assumed it was all about the food and me having no self-control; but sometimes, ACTUALLY 99% of the time, it had to do with my mental health and wanting control over my life when I couldn't control the world's opinions of me, how my parents treated me, my self-loathing or my sexuality.

Great—the art of masking diet culture and marketing it as a path to happiness, a perfect life, and lifetime fulfillment. BEAUTIFUL. I'm being sarcastic, if you couldn't tell already.

Welp, here I am, maybe in the third grade by now, internalizing the self-hatred everyone projected. I took it on as my own, learning that it was not okay to be in a bigger body, not okay to show emotion, and not okay to be myself. Internalizing the opinions of others led me to develop negative beliefs about myself and my body.

The meaner I was towards myself, the more negative energy and anger I projected into the universe. I took the negativity in my life, in any form it came, and blamed it on my weight. Negative core beliefs I had planted into my brain held on firmly, leading me to believe I was inherently born a worthless and bad person.

Don't get me wrong, I wanted to be horizontal and cry every day because the kids at school would poke fun at my high-pitched voice and my weight. Like, bitch, I cannot control when my balls drop. Or I guess you could call it puberty? Whichever you prefer.

However, I couldn't tell my parents that I was being bullied at school, nor did I trust them enough to tell them the things I was struggling with. I kept it all bottled up, even when I got home. I couldn't be sensitive at home or I would've been scolded and scrutinized as "less of a man." Seriously, who said I wanted to be a man anyway?

Sometimes the lessons you learn from your parents are what stick with you for a long time and can bleed into your adulthood. It did for me. I learned to never show emotion because it meant that I was weak, less than my peers, and would be more prone to issues. Later on in life, I unlearned this lesson through therapy. But hold your horses, doll, I'll get to it.

But first, what are some of the lessons you learned from your parents? They can be good too. I'm hoping that not everyone faced as much trauma as me.

CHAPTER FIVE

Dean vs. Dicks

So, being an in-the-closet gay that I was and having family pressure me into being a "man," I naturally fell into a relationshit—I mean, relationship. Let's call her Valerie (that obviously was not her actual name). I don't want to expose anyone besides myself. Again, ya girl cannot afford to be in more debt.

Valerie and I met in the chorus club, but trust me, I cannot sing to save my life. Seeing each other in chorus rehearsals and all, we became friends and started talking more on AIM/AOL. This was during the time AIM or AOL was poppin'. Let's just put it this way: when you go out of your way and force yourself to like someone, it's probably equivalent to not knowing whether you need to poop or fart. If you force it, honey, it's probably shit. Valerie was my first and last relationship. Oops.

Our relationship was always on and off. I know! I should've seen the signs, but I was dealing with other shit, okay?! Well not that there was REALLY a relationship to begin with. Maybe a friendship? I don't mean that in a bad way. I just don't think we knew what we wanted or had figured out who we were yet. We were just some kids trying to survive. Please don't drag me; I know it sounds like a cheesy romantic comedy film.

I think that's what made us perfect for each other at that time. As youngins, we would sneak around trying to see each other without our siblings or parents noticing. I remember the cringe moments where the majority of our relationship took place online. Yes, we did change our Aim statuses the day we "got together." Which, now that I think about it, was a RED FLAG! One time we made out at her front door and her brother saw. It was one of the weirdest moments of my life. Girl, it wasn't because I was almost caught by her brother; it was because I was HELLA turned off. Yikes.

I. WAS. CONFUSION.

Being confused is great though. I think it makes you question a lot about yourself, and it helps you to invest in yourself. Except I was confused and also dealing with a million other things. I was still struggling mentally, and my self-esteem was not improved just because I was dating a girl. It might've been masked but definitely not dealt with.

But of course, the more confused I was, the more the universe wanted to help me find out the answer. And you know what the universe said to my family? Let's TAKE A FAMILY VACATION back to China!

GURL, I was triggered. A wave of emotions came floating back to me because it felt so familiar, yet distant. I hadn't seen my grandma or aunt since I was four and a half, and I was scared of their opinions and how they would treat me. I was so used to family and friends calling me "fat" and "chubby" in America that automatically, my negative self-talk changed the way I experienced reuniting with my grandma and aunt. I didn't want to feel any of these negative emotions, so what do I turn to? You guessed it, queen: FOOD.

It irritated me that everyone around me kept commenting on my weight, especially those in China who claimed to love me but complained that I was more obedient when I wasn't "like this." Okay, so how are you going to accept just some parts of me? This frustration caused me to be a "rebel" in my mind and continue shoving food down my throat to prove everyone right. I thought, if y'all are stressed about my weight, I will take revenge by eating even more food, just to confirm that I was worthless, lazy, and an unlovable kid who at first glance was always insulted and made fun of.

Of course, my family did not give two shits about how I felt. So, what did they decide to do? Go to a pool! A literal worst nightmare for any kid struggling with their body. Naturally, existing in a body that I was TAUGHT to hate living in, I chose to wear oversized extra-large T-shirts that were preferably non-translucent when wetting. I wish I had a "do not wet" sign to stick to my back, cause UGH! Little did I know, people in China were actually meaner and extremely blunt about how they felt about MY body.

Two security guards came up to me one day at the swimming pool. They were LAUGHING, asking me how much KFC I had eaten to get this big. They assumed I was "disgusting" and a "pig" because of my body. Bitch. First of all, don't comment on anyone's body. Second of all, why would you go out of your way to make me feel bad at a swimming pool when I was clearly insecure and trying to hide? I just don't get people sometimes. Anyway, I felt so ashamed and felt a hole in my chest. I felt like the water was choking me, but it was probably all the tears I had been holding back my whole life.

It's whatever. People living in China have their own issues to deal with. Thinness was advertised everywhere and bombarded the Chinese citizens. Myself included. The more exposed I was to fatphobic messages, the more ashamed I felt about my body, and the more I binge ate. See the correlation? It's crazy how vivid I remember some moments.

I remember staying at my grandma's some days and staying at hotels other days. I constantly binged on these shrimp burgers from a fast-food chain. Dickies I think was the name. I KNOW. The world was trying to tell me something. They just tasted so good to me that I would eat maybe five in one sitting. Ugh, what I would do to go back and tell little Dean that the burger probably did not even taste good after the third one. He didn't know how to cope! But no, I wouldn't take these experiences back because LESSONS, baby.

Although thinness, white beauty standards, and material values were being advertised, that's not the only thing I took from my China visit. Remember when I said I had to go to the pool? Yeah well, there was one thing I did not mention to you.

The. Locker. Rooms.

Okay, gays, calm down. I know it's a scary term for the young version of us. As ashamed and as ugly as I felt, I still somehow managed the courage to use the locker room, but I was obviously covered for the most part. I literally saw dicks flopping around because it was a naked-locker-room-type situation. Apparently, in China, everyone was comfortable doing that.

This was one of the first sexual awakenings I experienced in my life. Someway, somehow, my brain finally allowed me to notice that I was into men. After that, there was literally no turning back. I'd always felt weird tingly feelings around men, but never like this. I never knew how to describe it. But after being exposed to the not-so-PG-13 part of my trip—the Chinese locker rooms—I knew.

I think I like boys. My friend down there agrees with me.

I know, I know what you're thinking. Did Dean really just see some random dicks flopping around and now he's into dicks? Girl, maybe. My life was not the same after realizing these feelings came about when I was most vulnerable. When my insecurities and anxiety got to me from the cops at the pool (who are trash, by the way), I cried. I haven't cried in a while, so I think crying released some room in me for new experiences. Hence seeing the dicks and realizing… yup! That's my life!

Returning to the United States, I was more conscious of not only my body but how I presented to the world. Because now I felt more pressure to be someone—anyone—as long as it wasn't myself.

I started to notice my sexual tendencies shifting from what I was taught as acceptable. I started to feel less attraction to girls, and the thought of dating Valerie at this point… was just, no. Valerie and I had been on and off for about two years, but as I said before, we were just kids who didn't know what we wanted. I was a whole mess, and didn't know how to manage my emotions, forcing myself to like girls even after realizing I was into men.

Sorry, Valerie. If you're reading this, know that I still love you (as a friend though, haha). I'm happy for Valerie and me: the universe made us stronger and unique because we got to explore parts of ourselves with each other. At the end of the day, it all worked out. She turned out lesbian, I turned out gay.

TEA. Surprise, bitch!

Well, also considering the fact that she was really into basketball and sports—meanwhile, the thought of sports to me… let's just say you'll never find me at a sports bar unless it's a gay sports bar. Okay, at that age, probably not a bar and more like my dad's porn stash. Every dad has a porn stash…right?

After that sexual awakening I had, literally nothing was the same! *Cue Drake song.* I was snooping around like the nosy Sagittarius I am; that's when I first find my dad's porn stash. Other kids would've been like "EEEEEW, gross!" But me? Nope. What's new though? I was curious when I found them, and I don't know why I expected to find a gay porn disc. Ugh, wishful thinking.

CAN YOU IMAGINE? I would've lost my shit.

At this point, I did not really identify with any sexual orientation. I just knew men made me feel ways that women couldn't. Even before my sexual awakening in China, I was intrigued by girls. My friends always tell me how weird it is coming from me. Honey, I know! But that just proves the point that sexuality is indeed FLUID!

No matter how sexually fluid, open-minded, and nice I was, I always felt judged because kids scared me. They still scare me.

When was your last sexual epiphany? Awakening? Write down moments you remember that changed your view on people you are attracted to.

___

Who were they? How have they changed or stayed the same?

___

CHAPTER SIX

High School (Not) Musical

As I was applying to high schools, I tried to aim for the best schools, but you guessed it! Rejected from my top three choices. Townsend Harris, Bard Early College, and Francis Lewis High School. New York City had this weird system where they made you apply to twelve schools using a directory instead of automatically going to your zoned school. But me being me, I was doing my high school application last minute, so I ended up looking at all the graduation rates of schools and putting down random schools for the rest.

In March of 2011, I got a letter in the mail that said, "Congratulations! You've been accepted into Aviation Career & Technical High School."

"What the fuck?"

I had no idea where this school was and more importantly, I did not know what aviation even meant. After some research, I had an **ANXIETY** attack because I found out that the school had over 70% boys! Probably the closest I got to crying over something school-related. In-the-closet me started to overthink and beat myself up for not taking high school applications more seriously. Before even giving Aviation High School a chance, I started appealing, but I ended up going anyway.

My biggest fear was being bullied for being more feminine than the rest of the boys at school. And don't get the wrong picture. This wasn't your typical high school experience. Now that I live in Los Angeles, I know what the movies view as a high school. In New York City, you do not have a huge football field, track, and a parking spot when you're 14!

To be fair, I would not have used the football field or track anyway. No, not because I was in a bigger body. Just the thought of being in a locker room full of sporty, masculine, and straight men SCARED me. I could barely change in front of people in gym class, let alone for sports. I wanted high school to be a fresh start for me because I had grown up and spent elementary and middle school with the same people.

Even if ya girl wanted a fresh start, the "unacceptable" and "overweight" body that I was living in did not allow others to see me in any other way except as the fat kid who was easy to push around.

The truth of the matter is, it was so much more than my weight. Thinking back to the moment I started at Aviation, I did not have the fresh start I so wanted. I didn't make new friends or fit in. Not because I was in a weight stigmatized body—ok, maybe some of it has to do with that since our society praises those in thinner/smaller bodies. Thinking about it from a more rational perspective, the things I wanted couldn't happen because how could I expect others to be receptive and loving when I didn't even like myself? Trust me, when you don't like yourself, the vibes you give off—people can feel them. I was angry all the time, mad at the world, and every single night, I would pray to wake up in a different body and straight.

That obviously did not happen. The more I hated myself and lashed out in anger towards those around me, the more isolated I felt.

High school was one of the loneliest times of my life. I fell into a mundane routine where I would go to school, have kids at my school greet me as, "What's up, Chubby?" and then buy a bunch of McChicken's afterschool at the McDonalds a block away so I could go home and numb out. My binge eating got extremely out of hand, but did I care?

No.

Binge eating, food, and self-hatred were my only friends who made me feel like I was in control of my life. At the time, I felt these destructive behaviors served a purpose: helping me not kill myself. I never let anyone know how I was feeling at school or what I was dealing with, and I blamed myself constantly.

The more I figured out my sexuality and who I was interested in, the more I wanted to stay in the closet. I always heard homophobic comments in high school, and all the boys would slap each other's asses, proceeding with, "No homo." First of all, you should get consent before touching anyone, and second of all, I didn't even do that. But here these little high school boys go, spreading rumors about me and asking the people slightly acquainted with me if I was gay.

Honey, maybe if you asked me, I would've told you the truth? Ok no, not really. But if you're reading this and in high school, I hope you treat everyone with the kindness you want to be reciprocated to you. I want to shout out to those who were kind to me even when I didn't like myself.

I always felt lonely and felt that I had no friends, but I'd like to thank the few gems who made life a bit easier to handle in a school full of toxic energy. I felt nervous and uneasy. I know, I know, I said before that I didn't have any friends. But I think with the mindset I had in the past, my trust issues, and all the shit I was dealing with, I couldn't rationalize that someone could actually be my friend.

That's why I always say, keep the ones who were there for you or befriended you at your worst and stay in touch with them, because when you work on yourself, the **FAKES** will jump out. I don't know about you, but I'd rather have 4 quarters (real friends) than 100 pennies (the fakes).

Nearing the end of my first year, I was at the heaviest I had ever been. The doctors were really concerned about my well-being and constantly tried to put me on diets. But surprise! **DIETS DON'T WORK!** They only make you feel worse about yourself.

I hated going to the doctor because every time I went, it reinforced that I was an outcast, heavier than most people my age and that I had to change in order to be happy, accepted, and loved. There was one time I went to the doctor and they told me if I didn't start starving myself, losing weight, or exercising, I would have to draw a pint of blood every single month to "maintain" my weight. Little did the doctors know how much their words impacted my relationship with food.

With that much power, I always questioned doctors. Instead of making children and the general population feel bad about themselves if they don't fit the "weight" or "BMI" chart, why didn't they use their power to teach parents to love their child no matter what they look like? I'm not saying go feed your kid twenty slices of cake, but working on the mental issues before the food will allow for long-term happiness.

After numerous doctor visits, I knew what to expect every single time. It was always the same feedback. I needed to lose weight. So much so that my mom sat me down one night and told me if I lost weight, she would buy me a 2,000 dollar laptop. Of course, at this point in my life, I felt like I needed to do anything to gain her approval, love, and support so that maybe, just maybe, she would accept my queerness if I came out to her. I knew my parents had homophobic tendencies because I remember one random Sunday when my sister, my mom and I were walking down the streets of Chinatown.

My sister randomly asked, "Mom! What if Dean is gay?"

Without any hesitation and with a voice full of judgment, she said, "Then he would be crazy."

My parents were extremely traditional and strict, so I always wanted to gain their approval, even if it ended up with them yelling at me for not doing enough. But I'm telling you right now, doing things and seeking approval from others will give you temporary happiness, but that happiness will soon fade.

In the summer of 2012, I started an exercise program that lasted two months. It came with at-home exercise videos and a two-month calendar to keep you on track. I was too insecure, ashamed, and scared to sign up for a gym membership, but I think I wasn't even old enough to sign up anyway.

...and so it began.

I started weighing myself every day to make sure I was making progress and that I would attain that 2,000 dollar laptop. But more importantly, so I would gain approval from the world and maybe even my parents. It was my life's mission to be seen, heard and accepted.

During this two-month program, I realized how much I hated forcing my body to work out when I didn't want to. This is when I forgot how to listen to my body and started ignoring the hunger cues it gave me. I learned not to trust my body because it was "my body's fault" that I was overweight, unaccepted, and unhappy. Boy, was I wrong. It was another outlet for me to blame my life's traumas.

In the first month of working out, I still binge ate most of the time until I learned and forced myself to restrict. I saw no progress in the way I looked, so in the second month, I made a promise to myself to push even harder, even if that meant starving myself. I remember crying over the bathroom scale, weighing myself on every scale in the house, and going to sleep hungry. I firmly believed this was the golden ticket and the way out of the darkness I'd experienced in my life.

Slowly but surely, I started to feel anxiety around situations dealing with food. This was just the start, so I didn't catch it. In hindsight, I wish I did. I will always remember those nights I would lie to myself and those around me that I was "full," saying I had already eaten something.

My parents were overjoyed to see that I was able to "control" myself for the first time in my life. I didn't know who I was or what I was doing, but I knew one thing for sure: I needed to keep losing weight. I needed to "prove" my haters wrong. I needed to change so I could finally be happy. In reality, I was always okay, and my weight did not make me a worse person; it was the mental baggage, abuse, and trauma that made it an easier outlet to blame/control.

What has diet culture taught YOU? I want you to think of things you hear that are directly related to diet culture in your everyday life and write them down. How are you going to reject those messages and protect your self-love?

CHAPTER SEVEN

O.M.G.
You're An Inspiration

When I finally lost almost half of me at the end of summer, after figuring out unhealthy ways to do so, I was praised for it. I came back to school a whole different person. But wait, you're probably wondering how much weight I lost? Nope. Girl, I will not be disclosing my weight because fuck triggering content. You do not need that, hun!

This was the first time my parents showed even remote proudness for any accomplishment in my life. My parents were so proud of me for "finally losing weight" and for finally taking care of myself. They bragged to all their friends and family in China and told me I finally looked good. After gaining their acceptance just a little, I felt euphoric. I felt like I was finally seen by the people who birthed me—the ones who are meant to love me for who I am. Period.

When school started back up again, I was nervous yet excited at the same time. Nervous more so because I was still hiding the fact that I was gay and had developed the beginnings of an eating disorder. The number of times I prayed to buddha (because my family would go to temple on Sundays) to turn me straight didn't do anything, so… is buddha canceled? JUST KIDDING! I was stuck in the mindset that homosexuality could be cured. I mean, perks of growing up in a traditional, homophobic household, right?

On the first day of sophomore year of high school, I walked into school looking like another person, but I was the same person on the inside—traumas and all. From having no attention to having random people come up to me, I felt validated and seen for once. People who could care less about me and never talked to me when I was overweight came up to me saying how proud they were—proud that I learned to take care of my health and lose weight.

This taught me to focus on external validation and to equate happiness to the way I looked. On the outside, I was thriving, an inspiration, and a role model because of my "discipline." I was literally the same person as I was before. Ugh, shallow bitches.

But now that I was in a "better" and a more acceptable body, people wanted to be associated with me. On the inside, I knew I had lost weight, but I also felt I had lost a part of me in return. I had this unique, quirky laugh but I lost it when I lost the weight.

The more people praised me and saw me as an inspiration, the deeper I got into my eating disorder. Because I struggled with binge eating disorder all my life, when I lost weight, no one questioned if I had an eating disorder. The world simply saw my external changes and didn't question if my mental health was okay.

When I took an existing eating disorder and did a complete 180, no one questioned. To the world, when you lose weight after living in an unacceptable body, you are graced with attention/praise. However, when you lose weight if you're already in an acceptable body, everyone is concerned and encourages you to get help.

With all this newfound attention, I was hyper-aware of everyone's judgments towards me. I became way more involved in school activities than ever before. I made friends in Robotics, clubs, and in my classes, but I always kept friendships more surface level, minus a few. It was hard for me to trust anyone around me because I was carrying deep and dark secrets that I wanted to remain hidden from the world.

After a while, the praise got old and I didn't feel like I was being validated anymore. This is when my repressed traumas crept back up on me. I tried my best to push them down by involving myself in school, track, and focusing on making more friends. But the real tea is, no matter how many "friends" I made, I still felt empty on the inside because I didn't even see myself as a friend.

CHAPTER EIGHT

I ~~Am Asian~~
Wanted to Be White

After joining Robotics, I met someone named Billie. No girl, not Billie Eilish. I WISH. Billie is a code name because I do not need him coming for my DMs or suing me. I'm trying to be debt-free, y'all.

So, when I first met Billie, he was extremely nice. I really connected with him because I felt somewhere deep down that he was probably also gay. Turns out, he was. He was also in the closet so that made me feel even closer to him because I could relate. Naturally, the first guy I know for sure is gay, I fall for. Literally, falling for men who are bad for me is my worst personality trait.

I start to overthink our friendship because the first guy I liked, shouldn't he know? How naive of my dumb sophomore year ass. Anyway, he was the first guy I had ever come out to, but I came out to him via AIM/AOL because doing it in person would've been too scary for me.

Quite frankly, that would be disappointing because coming out in my head was me strutting in seven-inch platform heels into the light (boy was I wrong, HAHA).

After I came out to him, this was the "honeymoon phase" of our friendship. He was the closest friend I had ever had in my entire life. He understood all the things I was going through in terms of my sexuality and living as someone in the closet. Billie gave me perspective about friendships and that you could actually trust people. His relationship with his best friend showed me that maybe people weren't as bad as they seemed. Let's call her Flow.

Everyone in school thought Billie and Flow were dating, but as an in-the-closet gay, that was perfect for him. I thought, did I need someone like that too? But no, as I said earlier, he showed me that you could trust people. It ain't mean I was able to trust that quickly. Trust issues don't go away overnight—one can only wish.

I felt like I belonged. Of course, his friends eventually became friends of mine. Like your typical romance story, I fell in love with him. OMG, no ew, just kidding. I tried being poetic for two seconds and nope. Okay, maybe I wasn't IN love with him; I just liked him a lot. It came to a point where we would text all the time, and he did make me smile. It wasn't serious by any means, but our friendship/closeness didn't really last when I told him how I felt.

I finally confessed to him that I liked him, but immediately after, it became awkward. We communicated through Flow, and we would sometimes have menial conversations.

I could tell he didn't like me back, so I shut him out like I always do with people who could potentially hurt me even more. Even then, I self-sabotaged because although I didn't want to get hurt more, what did I do? Asked Flow why he didn't want to date me or why he would never have feelings for me.

Facepalm.

This was when Billie and Flow changed my life—not in a good way.

When I asked Flow why Billie was keeping his distance, it took her a while to tell me. The conversation started out well and made me feel slightly validated.

"I don't know if I should tell you. Fuck it, I'll tell you anyway." I could tell Flow was nervous too, but I don't blame her. I would be nervous too.

"He said, 'Dean's a great conversationalist, funny, and a wonderful person to hang out with. But too bad he's Asian.'"

BITCH, I WAS FUMING.

I was livid at the situation and at him. I'm not saying I was or even felt like the hottest guy in the world, but having a "type" based on race? Sweetie, that just means you're racist—or you're going through some internalized racism.

But of course, at this point in my life, I saw the situation as the world was against me, so I immediately thought there was something wrong with me. Billie taught me that it wasn't okay to be myself, it wasn't okay to be Asian, and more importantly, things I could not change were the parts wrong with me. So, what did I do? Immediately try to change them.

King of a bad decision? You're looking at him right now.

What was one of YOUR worst decisions that allowed negative people into your life? Reflect.

_____

_____

_____

_____

_____

I continued to use food to numb because my eating disorder gave me the illusion of being in control of my life. Using disordered behaviors felt like I had an agency and a voice since I didn't have control over my ethnicity. I looked in the mirror every day, told myself I was ugly, worthless, and had to keep losing weight in order to gain acceptance.

I made sure every sound, vowel, and peep that came out of my mouth did not have hints of an accent. I really thought self-loathing and self-criticism was the path to success, happiness, and bettering myself. My goal was to look as un-Asian as possible.

I wanted to be white SO bad, and existing in this world did not make it easier. A majority of people believe they are the issue when in reality, capitalism profits off our insecurities so why would they stop promoting self-loathing/hate as a way to become better?

Once my anorexic tendencies stopped working, I searched online and found out how to eat without gaining weight. And surprise, there were pro-anorexia websites to encourage you to throw up when you binge.

The more I self-loathed and hated my ethnicity, the worse my eating disorder got. I felt like I was in control, but at the same time, I felt SO out of control. My mind was filled with thoughts of food and how I could manipulate my diet so I could be as thin as the white kids in school who seemed like they all had fast metabolisms.

It got to a point where my web engine search feed consisted of these topics:

How to be white and talk white
Eye-lid enhancement surgery
Eye color change from brown to blue surgery cost
Lowest calorie foods
Empty calorie foods
I can't throw up anymore, how to keep vomiting

Some kids at school started becoming concerned for me, but I didn't give a fuck. My eating disorder took over my thoughts, and I felt like anything anyone ever did was done against me. Even nice things. I thought the thinner I got, the more power I had over everyone because it was something they couldn't achieve.

I wanted to graduate so I could leave this family, leave this town, and leave this school. I was constantly hungry, so naturally, I was lashing out to everyone around me, regardless of how small the situation was. I would lie to everyone around me, telling them that I kept a strict exercise regimen, ate healthy food, and controlled my portions!

Every morning, I woke up at 4 am and lied saying I needed to study. Well, I was studying but I was mostly binge eating, spitting out my food, and throwing up. I was consumed. I was an addict. I was broken. I would pretend to be happy and fine when I went to school.

Meanwhile, every night at dinner, I would be starving because I had dropped lunch off my schedule. I was my biggest competitor. I made sure to eat dinner really quickly with my parents and then go purge right after to prevent weight gain.

So essentially, I was starving 24/7. The hungrier I was, the more accomplished I felt.

The less Asian I felt.

The less me I felt.

The less sadness I felt.

The feeling of euphoria came from the fact that I was going insane, I was malnourished, and I didn't have enough energy to think about or even feel any uncomfortable feeling.

I felt powerful with my eating disorder. I thought, HA! I'm stronger than all of you. I can maintain my weight even though Google told me I'd gain it all back! Even my parents were a bit concerned. But I did not give a fuck. I would argue back to them because weren't they the ones who wanted me to lose weight in the first place? Weren't they the ones who forced me to lose weight? I used my eating disorder as a tool for rebellion. The more they said I was too skinny, the more weight I lost. I hated myself and blamed them. I blamed the world and how the universe did me wrong in every way.

I wanted to escape, so I did.

Has anyone in your life said something so unforgivable that it changed the way you view/viewed yourself? Let out everything you want to say to that person. Analyze the insecurities they may have that caused them to project onto you.

_____
_____
_____
_____
_____
_____
_____
_____
_____
_____
_____
_____
_____
_____
_____
_____
_____
_____
_____
_____
_____
_____
_____

Now, Repeat after me:
I love myself despite the false judgements of others.

CHAPTER NINE

Bye, Queens!

To be completely honest with you, I don't know how I just took my bags and left, but I'm so glad that I did. I used my last few years in high school perfecting my escape plan, and I don't mean running away from home: I moved away for college.

I purposely applied for Occidental, the school I ended up attending. I knew I wanted to live in Los Angeles for as long as I can remember. I fantasized about living a free life since I realized the cards I was dealt in life. I guess TV shows and films really portrayed Hollywood in a way that convinced me, more than my parents ever could.

They wanted me to stay in New York City so badly. They wanted to "keep an eye" on me so I didn't turn into a disappointment, even though I already felt like one living under the same roof as them. Nothing they could say or do could take back the way they treated me growing up, and I knew in my heart that my decision was made.

There was no looking back. Queens was my home, still is. Forever. However, you best believe that I needed to get the FUCK out of there.

I convinced myself that moving to Los Angeles, away from all the negativity, childhood trauma, and the place where my eating disorder originated, would solve all my problems overnight.

This wasn't the case.

Part of me knew that moving to California was a way that I tried to escape from the people concerned about my weight, sexuality, and habits. I remember that I was still deep in my eating disorder, and all I could think about was food and about moving to a place where I could practice these destructive behaviors away from people who would prevent me from doing so.

It was an addiction.

I was still angry at the world, angry at myself, and very mentally unstable in my own terms. The only thing masking all that was a life change, but I was the king of hiding my emotions, so that wasn't hard.

However, I am so glad I made the impulsive choice to leave Queens, New York. If I hadn't, maybe you wouldn't even be reading this right now.

I was a fall baby, so my birthday was towards the end of November. Yeah girl, I was still 17! And if y'all think I look young now, imagine how I looked before. Perks of having a baby face, I guess. Thank whatever power vested in the universe that didn't write the trauma in forms of aging on my face… HA.

When I flew into LAX, I remember feeling everything and nothing at the same time. I felt excitement, joy, and genuine happiness for my future. Meanwhile, I also felt heartbroken, empty, and nostalgic. See, that's the thing about clinging onto the past. When I moved across the country alone with no family,

I started to get reflective about my life.

For those of you who watched *Gossip Girl*, I felt like Serena when she looks out the train window, reflecting on her life. Yep. Me.

Anywho, I started to fantasize, and my thoughts started romanticizing my past. Even the traumas!

Your mind can play tricks on you, where it makes you think for a second, "Ah, those were the days!"

No, those were not the days, honey (well, not for me at least). I don't think I had the ability to be present in the moment. I didn't give myself enough credit for hopping on a plane to go somewhere unknown, so my brain tried tricking me, trying to let my horrible past take away from my present. But, TEA!

I really felt like partying in the USA when I landed at LAX. Yes, I'm talking about Miley Cyrus's song. I literally hopped off the plane with a dream and a cardigan—plus maybe a lifetime worth of trauma, but at least no more seasons!

I came out immediately when I got to Occidental College, and that was the first healthy step I took to glitter my way into the person I am today. I felt a weight lifted off my shoulders because I didn't have to hide who I was anymore.

Well, to be fair, it wasn't easy at first because it took some adjusting. I think after a few months, I stopped looking over my shoulder or being cautious of being myself. And for those of you who think coming out or making huge life changes will solve all the things you're dealing with mentally... Girl, let me TELL you.

Coming out did not solve my issues with weight, how I felt about myself, my negative core beliefs, my internalized racism, self-hate, and the list goes on. My traumas still cut me deeper than a knife because mental health, eating disorders and life isn't as simple as that.

Moving 3,000 miles and across the country can't magically

heal wounds—I should've known that. I was the smallest I'd ever been and the unhealthiest I'd ever been. My hair was bleached and literally looked like one of those hay-like brooms.

I just dragged myself, but whatever. I wore blue contacts every day so I could trick everyone into thinking I was not Asian. Maybe mixed or white, but DEFINITELY not Asian.

The words Billie and Flow said to me stuck with me, traveled from NYC to LA with me, and still affect me somewhat till this day. But the beautiful thing in the not knowing is that moving away from home allowed me to start working on these broken pieces inside me, one by one.

What are some risks that you have taken? What risks haven't you taken because of that little voice in your head? Write it all down honey.

HEALING

CHAPTER TEN

Therapy, Who Is She?

I'm not sure if it was the same for all of you, but I remember growing up and not really learning about mental health or even acknowledging it. Partly, I think it was because my parents grew up in China. If you grew up in a traditional Chinese household, or any strict traditional household, you get what I mean.

Mental health did not exist to them, and so I grew up always thinking something was wrong with me. I didn't have the skills or coping mechanisms to analyze the state of my mental health, let alone recognize mental health might've been the reason I'd been struggling my whole life. It never occurred to me that I might need therapy, so when I was introduced to therapy, mental health, and self-help, I was confused. Kinda shook too.

Mental health? Who? I never knew her.

It was invisible to me, and my family thrived off of suppressing emotions, and then taking them out in different parts of their life (aka their kids). Honestly, I know that I complained about how I struggled in college, but I'm glad they introduced me to this resource that I could get for free. I literally cannot imagine if they had charged for therapy, because I would NOT have been able to go. Remember? Hopped off the plane with zero-dollar signs! Well, technically it was because I was on financial aid. Thank GOODNESS, girl!

I don't know what my brain was on, maybe the endorphins from starving? No, I'm just kidding. Maybe endorphins from moving to California. You know when you're suddenly so motivated to do something? It was an impulsive feeling, but a feeling I am so grateful for to this day.

I wanted to stop dying so badly, but I was scared to go into my first therapy session. So, if you have friends who are afraid to go into their first therapy consultation, ask them if they want you for extra support! Same goes for if you are going; try to reach out because having someone is always comforting.

My first therapy consultation was the key to finally taking care of myself, molding myself, and finding who I truly was. My therapist's name was Matt. If you are reading this, thank you. Thank you for all that you've done and more. You are a blessing that I didn't realize I needed. Also, sorry for all the times my eating disorder wanted me to lie to you.

ANYWAY, I should've probably saved that thank you for the end, but I couldn't wait. I'm impatient, okay? I just want to tell people how much they did for me and affected my life!

Matt helped to start my mental health journey. He taught me ways to break down my traumas, even on my worst days. Even though it was difficult for me to open up, I knew that I had a problem…which is always the first step, right?

I always thought of myself as broken. So broken that nothing in this world could fix me, nothing could take away the trauma, and nothing would change.

Well, I was partly right. Nothing in this world can take away any trauma, but you can learn to deal with it and nourish your past so you can have a bright future.

What has therapy done for you? What have you learned? If you have never gone to therapy, what is stopping you? What are your fears about therapy?

I don't know what it was about Matt, but from the moment I met him, I immediately felt like I could open up about my issues. Okay, probably because he said everything was confidential. But EVEN then, I was skeptical. Trust issues, girl; I knew her too well.

After I admitted to him that I thought I had an eating disorder, to make the blow less harsh towards myself, I was able to unleash all the other traumas that I had kept inside ('cause tea, we never REALLY want to face our challenges head-on if we are struggling). I talked about my childhood, eating struggles, childhood separation, and my self-induced hatred about my ethnicity.

The hard part about all of this was, I admitted to all my traumas and tried to piece my life together, work on my issues, and use coping skills. None of them really worked for me. I was resisting.

No matter how much tea I spilled, how much I vented, and how much I WANTED so bad to heal, I always found excuses as to why I couldn't go to treatment. Matt, like the angel therapist he was, even helped me call eating disorder programs that were in-network for student health insurance. We talked through a bunch of them, and the best financially affordable one for me was the Bella Vita.

Even after deciding on the Bella Vita, I was reluctant to go. I was so fucking stubborn that I used any excuse I could find.

"Oh, I can't afford it, I can't miss school, I can't miss work, and I don't have the time."

BULLSHIT!

All these things were irrelevant. By irrelevant I mean in relation to the position I was in at this time in my life. I wanted to heal but I didn't. I was stuck in this cycle where one day, I would want to go and then the next, I would change my mind.

I didn't realize that health was the most important thing amongst all. Everything else could come after health because if you don't nourish a body that tries so hard to keep you alive, you have nothing. No amount of money, fame, grades, or praise would matter if you dropped dead—at least that's what I told myself to push myself into treatment.

After this tug-o-war between my eating disorder's voice and Matt, that sliver of hope inside me finally agreed to go to an initial consultation at the Bella Vita. I was scared. I was afraid the coping skills I had known and had used throughout my childhood and teen years would vanish and I would be left with the weight of the world in my chest.

CHAPTER ELEVEN

Losing My Rehab Virginity

The Bella Vita was really close to my school, which made it harder for me to make excuses as to why I couldn't attend. Because at this point, I still didn't have a car. Well, to be fair, I still don't have a car.

I'm A PROFESSIONAL PASSENGER, OKAY?

I will say that until the day I get my license. But we'll see when that is, 'cause, girl, I'm convinced I can't drive.

After my consultation, they decided to place me into intensive outpatient three times a week when I didn't have classes because I was so adamant about staying in school and not falling behind. Deep down, I knew this was not the level of care I needed. I didn't want to admit it because I knew they would listen and take me out of school.

Lord, I need to go back and smack some sense into 17-year-old Dean. I didn't REALLY want help at this time. I didn't think I deserved it. I thought of eating disorder treatment more as a burden, which was a testament to me feeling like a burden to everyone around me, just reflected and projected in a different way.

My eating disorder manipulated me and convinced me to take the path of least resistance, which included skipping treatment days and making false excuses. Here I was spending days in treatment, just to spend as many, if not more, days undoing all my progress and engaging in my destructive behaviors. The amount of times I missed treatment because of continued eating disorder behaviors and fear of facing the unknown—well, I can't even count how many.

When I did show up for treatment, I was always nervous for weigh-in day. I remember secretly forcing myself to drink **GALLONS** of water before going into treatment so it would seem like I was "recovering." My dumbass didn't even stop to think that these were eating disorder professionals. They had been in this field and knew how to watch your every move. If I'm being honest, every single nutritionist I met with I hated.

The disordered thoughts in my head kept screaming, "DO NOT TRUST THEM! They're just trying to make you fat!"

"Am I a fraud?" I kept asking myself that question over and over again as I went to treatment every day, not wanting to be there.

Truth is, I wasn't a fraud, even if I felt like one. I just wholeheartedly believed that I did not deserve to recover from my eating disorder, did not deserve love, and was not deserving of anything good.

Every time the scale went up, the more I pretended to be recovered and the more I believed I was inherently bad. My anxiety of gaining weight clouded the spark in me to want to recover. My disordered eating got worse and worse the more I tried to get out of treatment days. I would binge and purge until three in the morning, go to the gym, and wake up with absolutely no energy. I was killing myself slowly.

But like, bitch, what did you expect? To have so much energy? Sorry, I had to drag myself. The funny thing is, I thought I was so clever in all of this. I thought I was "getting away" and outsmarting the system. But at the end of the day, I was literally playing myself and self-sabotaging.

My nutritionist knew that I was still struggling and wanted to place me on a higher meal plan. That seemed like the worst thing in the world to me, and trust me, it was at the time—or so my eating disorder had me believe.

It was like whenever things got hard for me, I didn't want to feel. The higher my meal plan went, the more I missed treatment. See a correlation there? Three days became two, and two days became one. Until one day, I just stopped going all together and checked myself out of the Bella Vita. Probably not a smart choice. But hey, everything happens for a reason… yeah?

Have you ever self-sabotaged and felt down on yourself after? If so, how did that make you feel? Write these instances down, and for every action, write the opposite—something that will benefit your mental/physical health. The next time you have these urges to replicate these self-sabotaging behaviors, look back to what you have written down.

_____
_____
_____
_____
_____
_____
_____
_____
_____
_____
_____
_____
_____
_____
_____
_____
_____
_____
_____
_____

Looking back, I really wasn't ready to give up my eating disorder. After quitting treatment and falling even deeper into my eating disordered patterns, I felt more and more like a failure. I thought being popular in college would change everything and solve the emptiness I felt inside. The past repeating itself? You betcha, girl. I went back to using validation as a temporary fix to the void I felt.

College became a difficult time for me because I kept jumping from friend group to friend group but complained about "having no friends," and I blamed other people for my own misery. What I didn't see, and can see now, is that I was so broken.

I was giving off negative energy to people and was essentially asking them, "PLEASE FUCKING FIX ME."

GIRL, that is a lot to ask of someone. I'm going to spill the piping hot tea. Sometimes, you might be the problem, and I know it is hard to hear, but someone had to say it.

In my struggle to find stability in college, the problem, for the majority of the time, was me. Not because I was inherently bad like I believed, but because I didn't have any self-worth or stability inside. I had a void that was so deep, it needed so much love, nourishment and care. I didn't love myself, not one bit, so how could I expect others to love me back the way I wanted?

When I was starving, full of trauma and full of hatred, I was extremely sensitive to any type of obstacles or confrontation that came my way. Anything that challenged my negative core beliefs made me lash out. No matter how much love people showed to me, I always found reasons to negate that and ended up having a falling out with them.

Trust me, I was not pleasant to be around. I snapped at anything and everyone because I was so malnourished. Think of being **HANGRY**, and now multiply that by 24 hours, seven days a week. That's why my advice to anyone who lashes out at them is to not take it personally, because the other person is projecting their own insecurities and issues. In this case, I had to push the blame to others, but in reality, it was me who was unable to form these close relationships I craved, because I hadn't yet found a loving and close relationship with myself, the true me.

I sound like a broken record, but I kept going back to my eating disorder whenever I felt any sort of discomfort.

I would tell myself, "SEE? You can't trust anyone or rely on anyone, and everyone is against you."

This was easier than confronting the pain and admitting that I needed a higher level of care and continued treatment.

In order to temporarily fill a void, something I kept hidden besides my eating disorder was my suicidal thoughts, depression, and my addiction to drugs. I didn't know what else to do because every time I stepped on the scale, it would stay stagnant. That was a scary word for me. I wanted the scale to keep going down but starving myself got too hard, so drugs became my new friend.

As I was slowly rotting away, I couldn't even look at myself in the mirror. I was slowly killing myself with my eating disorder and with drugs because I was too scared to end my life immediately. In my mind, suffering was my punishment for not being good enough and for not living up to the socially constructed standards from my parents and the world.

I want to go give that boy a hug right about now. I want to tell him it will all be okay and that letting people in won't hurt as much as he thinks it will. I want to help him take his walls down, teach him that the healing process hurts but it hurts so good. If you're reading this and struggling, I want you to help yourself—now.

No waiting for later.

Now.

CHAPTER TWELVE

Lord… Again? A-Fucking-Gain?

Ok girl, I know what you're thinking. Again? Yes. AGAIN. I went to treatment the second time after my therapist convinced me I should just stick the middle finger to my ego. So, I dragged myself into treatment and made a deal with them.

This time, I kind of knew the ropes to treatment, and the devil inside me (my eating disorder), was ready to fight back. Two weeks. That's all it took. No, I'm totally kidding. This isn't *Dear John*; two weeks was NOT going to change shit. Again, I put everything above my health. I told them I could only do treatment for two weeks; then I would heal and move on with my life. Oh, how naive.

This time, the therapists who did my intake were not surprised. They expected me to come back because I did not follow treatment the way someone who truly wants to heal does. Bella Vita suggested that I go into inpatient to stop the behaviors.

In my mind, I thought this was the golden ticket. Although I was scared shitless, somehow I convinced myself two weeks was going to undo my entire life's traumas.

Treatment was different this time. I couldn't go anywhere, I couldn't over exercise, and I was being watched like a hawk by the daytime/nighttime nurses. All that didn't give me anxiety, because of course, I found ways to break rules and exercise. Anyway, the thing that gave me the most anxiety was when they told us a chef was going to prepare food for us, so I was freaking out about what my next meal would be and what meal plan I was going to be on. The thought of opening up to a bunch of strangers also gave me anxiety. And may I point out, they were all women. Like okay, I've seen enough of this world to know men have eating disorders too, so stop assuming only women struggle!

Residential helped keep my anorexia and bulimia at bay, but I still did not understand why my eating disorder had developed. I still had not recognized that food was never the issue in the first place. Ironically, my biggest fear in residential was being "forgotten" at school. Something like "out of sight, out of mind." Of course, in group therapy, the staff would challenge me to analyze my fear of being forgotten.

Surprise! Ok, not really. This was just the tip of the iceberg. I was afraid of being forgotten because of my suppressed feelings of being "forgotten" as a child had manifested into my negative core beliefs—it shaped how I experienced and existed in the world.

Side note: after years of trauma, pain, and destructive behaviors, I'm pretty shook I still have teeth. Ok no, but for real. I was a fool to think two weeks could CURE my eating disorder… boy, was I wrong. I can tell you with full confidence, having been through the two-week residential program, that having a timeline for recovery will not be as beneficial to you in comparison to letting go and trusting.

Obviously, I convinced myself everyone was out to get me and that once I was healed, this place would be a distant memory. News flash: recovery was and is a lifelong process.

Think of a time when you were forced to let go and things turned out even better than you had imagined. How will you take steps to let go of things you have no control over, so you exude less stress/worry on yourself?

_____
_____
_____
_____
_____
_____
_____
_____
_____
_____
_____
_____
_____
_____
_____

CHAPTER THIRTEEN

I'm Back, Bitches!

After I got back to school from the "two weeks" of treatment, I felt "free." I literally left treatment acting like I was recovered, and deep down, I knew I felt free because I could go back to my old habits. I'll say it again. Having an eating disorder is extremely similar to having an ADDICTION.

Except, with food, you literally need it to survive; it's not something you can abstain from. Well, tea, I did abstain and that made me anorexic, so let's not do that.

It wasn't long before I started slipping back into old habits, even after I had promised myself after the two weeks I would not engage in any behaviors. I was behavior-free for maybe one day. Ok no, maybe 12 hours. Probably while I was in class.

I felt like I was in control of my life again after treatment had "taken it away," but I was just controlling it with food again. Feeling out of control and in control at the same time is something you get hit with in the gut. I lied to everyone, telling them I was recovered, and I even made posts on social media just to prove to everyone I was.

FAKE!

Slight drag to myself, but I'm sorry. I was a whole mess. Think clothes-on-floor-can't-walk-through-my-room type of mess times 100.

Here's the catch. I did this because I thought it would make others think highly of me. I didn't give a shit about how I felt. As long as I had approval from others, I felt fulfilled.

And sometimes when you're so broken, feeling fulfilled—even if it is for a split second—is something you grasp at desperately. I knew that I could die from my eating disorder, but if I could feel worthy for one second, it was enough.

My therapist was happy that I went to treatment twice, but he gave me his honest opinion about my recovery. That's why I love therapy. Sometimes they drag you, but you love it. Well, at least Dean loved it—my eating disorder, not so much. He tried so hard to get me back in treatment, giving me resources, options, and resolutions to my worries about leaving school.

My stubborn, Sagittarius, and scarred personality at the time kept fighting back. I made excuses for skipping treatment yet again. But this time, I told him that I didn't care if I died or got sicker; I had to finish school before going.

Horrible choice, Dean. Horrible.

You know how I said I always felt excluded, unlovable, and that no one cared for me? Well, whatever I forced myself to believe, I started to manifest into my life. Thinking about the times I felt excluded were always after I had canceled on plans so I could engage in my eating disorder.

The times I felt unlovable were always after I would lash out at everyone around me simply because I was STARVING. Gosh,

I was such a fucking bitch—a bitch who was starving and hangry all the damn time. TEA, but let's just leave that in the past.

The times I felt like no one cared for me were also times when my therapist showed care, but I actively rejected it. I rejected all these things I so wanted because I was blinded by my struggles, eating disorder, and trauma that made me believe I didn't deserve these things. After missing treatment, slowly but surely, I started to miss therapy sessions with Matt because I was afraid the more he knew about my struggles, the more he would take action and send me to treatment again. Even if it was what I needed at the time, I remember feeling scared—scared and ashamed I had to go back to rehab again.

At this point, my use of drugs to suppress my hunger, overexercising, and bulimia behaviors started affecting the one thing I kept making excuses for: school.

Remember when I said I couldn't go to treatment because I needed to finish school? Well, I was skipping class and skipping therapy so I could either exercise, count my calories, or binge and purge. Literally, I might be right back and hop in a time machine to ask past Dean–BOY, what is the truth?

Don't get me wrong, I was aware at times that I was slowly killing myself. But most of the time, I didn't really care. I pushed everyone away, especially those who genuinely cared about me. It was easier at the time to numb all my feelings rather than letting my walls down and getting help–again.

Because I was so adamant about finishing school, the disability services center worked with my therapist to create a plan for me. Even though the tea is that I wasn't even present in school. Girl, one time I was binging and purging all night and woke up late for a class presentation that I was speaking in. I felt really bad. I used to do my eyebrows every day, and let's just say I might've over done them. But obviously, I was rushing to this presentation, so I didn't really try to look good. This was probably the first time I left my dorm room looking casual, and my classmates asked me if I was sick cause I looked different. Ok, first of all, fuck y'all. Second of all, I'm kidding. However, yes, I WAS SICK! But I obviously couldn't tell them I was throwing up the night before. Can you imagine?

"Hey everyone, I have an eating disorder, so like, please give me attention and love, but I'll totally push you away."

OOP! I told you. I'm obnoxious and irritating, but that's how I cope, okay?! Using comedy and making fun of myself to this day is healing because for me, it places the irrational thinking, fears, and negative thoughts outside myself. Obviously, that didn't help heal my eating disorder, but you get what I mean. Like when I make jokes about my mental health, eating disorder, and struggles, it's fine. But when someone else tries to use them on me, I immediately ask whoever is around to hold my fucking earrings.

Anywho, because I'm nosy, what ways do you use comedy in your life? Do you use it to cope? How would you like to laugh more in life? And what makes you laugh the most?

CHAPTER FOURTEEN

Third Time's a Charm

As I was saying earlier, my therapist and disability services kept me "on track" so I wouldn't spiral out of control. That didn't happen. I spiraled out of control, even after they had provided me with everything. Simply because I did not want to heal. No matter how many people told me I needed to get help again, I didn't do it simply because I wasn't ready to commit to recovery. The more forced I felt to go to treatment, the further I pushed them.

In therapy, we tried to work on my habits, but nothing was working because my habits had been with me for so long. It's all I knew for a long time. My eating disorder disguised itself as the most beautiful relationship that I could never let go of, but in reality, it was an abusive relationship—a relationship that forced me into a darker and darker place.

Every time I had the chance, I wanted to please my eating disorder by following its "rules." I body-checked probably more than twenty times a day because I had extreme body dysmorphia. I had to make sure my arms, legs, and everything were the same size if not smaller.

It wasn't until one day, I started nose bleeding out of the blue that I thought something might be wrong. Well, that was the only sign I acknowledged. Because I was straight up in the DENIAL phase. Matter of fact, I was always cold, even when it was sunny outside, but I loved that feeling because I knew it meant that I was thin. I still can't wrap my head around what I was thinking. After I had that nose bleed, I told my therapist, and thank goodness. If I hadn't told him, I wouldn't have gone to get a physical done at the health center on campus.

After my results came out, my blood work showed signs of damage in my liver, kidneys, and my heart. My body was breaking down. Guess what your body starts to eat once all the nutrients are gone? It starts to eat your organs. I blamed my body at the time for being stupid and not knowing how to function.

In actuality, my body was trying to keep me alive while I was trying to torture it. I kept making excuses as to why my physical results came back poorly. Doing cocaine, drinking alcohol, and starving was not and never will be a good combination. Don't EVER do it, folks.

Did this scare the shit out of me? Hell yes, but I kept pushing myself to go another day until I "finished the semester." It wasn't until my therapist worked with the dean of students and my professors that I even considered going back to treatment. He made sure all the excuses were taken care of. And they were. I don't know what happened inside of me, but as treatment got closer, the more I opened up in therapy. I actually started tearing up a bit, which never happens. I had practiced being strong for so long. Strong enough so that nothing in the world could shake me, but what I needed to do was to let go and soften.

I was *scared*.
I was *ashamed*.
I was *broken*.
I was *dying*.

The days before I had to leave for treatment, I was in fight-or-flight mode. I was extremely anxious that this could be the last moments I could numb out and block out all feelings of pain—of sorrow. I couldn't stop binging and purging until the day I needed to be admitted.

CHAPTER FIFTEEN

May 10th, 2016

The worst and best day of my life. I was on the brink of death, while cleaning the fuck out of my dorm room. It was nasty because there were throw-up stains on parts of the walls.

My anxiety to go into treatment was ten-fold, but it made it easier for me to clean. As I was cleaning, my sister was texting me, asking if I was ready to enter rehab again for the third time. I took a moment to read our old conversations, where I was arguing with her and debating whether I should go to treatment or keep using destructive behaviors...

Thankfully, my anxiety helps me clean. I made sure that room was spotless. Cause girl, I needed to clean that dorm room because I could not afford to be in more debt.

"Well, are you ready?"

Brothers from the fraternity I was in offered to drive me to treatment. At that moment, I still felt like the world was against me, so I pretended I was okay, even if I could barely stand. I didn't need their pity. I didn't need anyone's pity. I was so close to running out of my dorm room and wanted to hide from the world so bad. I was bruised everywhere because I looked so gaunt that it was impossible for me to lay or sit anywhere besides my bed. I remember being unable to think after everything was packed, so I stared out into blank space, until I got a call from my sister.

Just seeing her name and photo appear on my phone, I already felt the tears coming. But no, I held it in. You know how awkward it was for me? Puh-lease. I know you prefer texting over phone calls too! Just kidding, I can't speak for everyone.

I probably LOVED texting because it meant I didn't really have to show my emotions, which was a skill I had mastered. When my sister and I ended up on the phone together, it was a moment you remember for life. There was a lot of silence. Not much back and forth until it got closer and closer to the time I had to leave.

It was nice to hear my sister's voice. It was a voice three thousand miles away, but it still felt close to my heart. Okay, that sounds very "in my feelings," but you get what I mean.

"Are you ready?"

My sister sounded concerned, but it was the first time I felt the pulse of warmth since moving away from home. To be real with you, I didn't know if I was ready. I didn't know if I was capable of giving up years of destructive behaviors in exchange for health. I know, it sounds crazy, but when you are as fragile as I was at this moment, it is when you need others to show you support. I was lost for words even to a simple question like that. I was broken.

"Please don't tell mom and dad. I need to do this."

I was desperate to run away from where my issues originated

and desperate to heal at the same time. This war inside me went on for so long, longer than I knew I was gay. And hun, that is a LONG time. My sister must have a sixth sense—knew to be mean to me 90% of the time, but somehow won me over 10% of the time. She is the most nourishing person I know, and as siblings, I know that even if we argue, we have an unconditional love for each other.

"I know, okay?" She sounded like she was holding something back.

"It's just, they've caused me so much pain, and I don't know if I can heal with them anywhere near me or knowing my whereabouts." I remember feeling afraid and unable to trust my own parents.

"I just need you to take care of yourself, okay? I didn't know most of my life that you struggled with things like this, and I feel like a shitty sister for not being there for you," she said, with her breath getting heavier and heavier.

My sister started sniffling. Eventually, she started crying. So naturally, I started crying. She made my heart break into a million pieces, but this time, my heart broke into a million pieces because of how loved I felt by her.

How did she know exactly what to say? I felt years of pent-up emotions come out and my chest felt heavy, even though I was a pile of bones. Okay, not ALL my emotions, but imagine a waterfall. Yeah, that was me.

My sister was in South Korea at the time studying abroad, so I didn't know if she was also in a room. All I know is that my back slid down the door. I sat there crying. I held my chest like I could not breathe.

This was the moment I knew.

I made a decision with the small light inside me and that little sliver of hope. I knew that even if this was a life-changing decision, I wasn't going to run. I knew that in order to be there for my sister, I had to be there for myself first. I had to live for myself.

My eating disorder had taken so much from me, and I could not let it take any more than what it had. I knew that if I let it, it would take my life next. I am so grateful that sliver of hope in me said NO.

Though it's different for everyone, I had to hit rock bottom before I went back to rehab. The deeper I got, the harder it was to come out of. This is why I'm telling you this, because if you are struggling with whatever is in your life, I don't want you to hit rock bottom and wait until it's too late.

CHAPTER SIXTEEN

Dean vs. ED

When I was dropped off at the Bella Vita treatment center in Thousand Oaks, I felt like I was in a movie. I felt like it wasn't real. This treatment center was a huge residential home and thank goodness, because I don't know if I would've focused on myself in a hospital setting. There were so many inspirational quotes and drawings around the house that gave the house a nurturing energy to the facility.

The second I was admitted, I met the other residents who were in the middle of group therapy. What caught my attention was the fact that there was finally one other guy in treatment with me. I was shook! The other times I went to treatment, whether it was outpatient or residential, there were no other male-identifying individuals.

Carter and I shared a room during my time in treatment, which I didn't get to experience the last time I was in residential. And no, that is not his real name. Y'all thought I would give you real names? I'm nosy TOO, but privacy! Anyway, the fact that he was also gay gave me a sense of hope. He had been there a few weeks before I was admitted, so he kind of guided me like a brother. Carter showed me that treatment is possible regardless of what addiction(s) you may deal with.

The other patients who were there when I entered treatment were Monica, Kendra, and Annie. I am so grateful for them because they showed me the ropes, showed me that recovery was in fact POSSIBLE, and that we were all in this together. Regardless of how different our past traumas were, I didn't feel judged because we were all just trying to deal with our shit and what life had thrown at us.

Obviously, it took me a while to trust them, but I think the honesty of the staff and journaling really helped me through. The only issue was that I felt like I was in a setting where I had to put up a front so people would not "dislike" me. Similar to how I viewed everyone and everything before I even got into treatment.

I remember a nurse, Jackie, was being extremely blunt with me after I did vitals one day. She asked me if I liked looking sick, like I was miserable, and being cold constantly. It hit my inner core, and that's when I turned that situation upside down. In my mind, obviously.

I felt like she was yelling at me, so I immediately wanted to be the "perfect patient." And trying to be perfect did NOT get me anywhere.

I was trying to be a perfectionist and didn't want to disappoint anyone or let anyone down, but the only person I was harming was myself! In the process of trying to "be the perfect patient," I sabotaged my recovery, by pretending to be happy, compliant, and in "recovery mode," when deep down, I didn't change the way I felt about my body, myself, and food, and I didn't let myself feel the pain of past traumas. Hence, why I couldn't deal with them and find new coping skills.

I tried to hide all my behaviors… once again. At night, when no one was around, I would sneak in the kitchen and binge eat whatever there was in the cupboards/refrigerator, feeling guilty and finding ways to binge/purge without anyone knowing. Until one day, a newly admitted resident, Jenna, joined the residential home with us, and told staff that she saw puke on the walls. I immediately felt like I had to put my guard up and try to lie my way into them believing me.

I ate at all the challenge meals, I would lie about my feelings, and I ate all my meals. I pretended to have a better mindset with all the staff, including the on-site psychiatrist and nutritionist. This went on and on, but I still didn't admit it to myself. I still tried to convince myself I was recovered enough to leave. The part of me that was so used to escaping kept trying to convince me to leave treatment.

The staff, especially the therapists and nurses, were probably SO annoyed at me. Lord, I would be annoyed with me too. I would bother them asking when my discharge date was because now that I had summer break, they didn't want to give me a discharge date. This was for the best, and looking back, I can see they wanted what was best for me. I was so focused on a discharge date that it held me back from dealing with my issues. It made me want to keep pushing down emotions and faking it until the day of my discharge.

I had constant racing thoughts and anxiety, but I didn't not tell my therapists or psychiatrist at the time. I was afraid of leaving treatment.

The perfect patient mentality went on for a while for me. After the head staff at the Bella Vita had announced to patients that there was food missing and put the blame on Kendra, whom

I had gotten close to… I felt bad, but my eating disorder did not allow me to be upfront.

I was able to convince them that I was still okay and the perfect patient, until they tested my blood and found an imbalance in my electrolyte levels. It took me one month to fully commit to recovery, because I wasn't fully recovering, even if my weight was going up. This was the longest I'd been in treatment. When the nurses and therapists finally caught on to my bullshit, I felt like I was having a panic attack, because my secrets had been revealed. I broke the rules the whole first month of treatment and lied to their faces that I was "fine." When they confronted me, asking me about binging, purging and missing food in the kitchen, the real Dean snapped out from the disordered voices, admitting to everything.

***

This moment was the turning point in my eating disorder recovery.

***

It was probably one of the first times I had felt exposed and vulnerable. I finally broke down for the first time since entering treatment. I was in shambles. This is when I realized that I was not perfect and I did not have to be perfect.

Recovery isn't *perfect*.
Recovery isn't *linear*.
Recovery isn't *easy*.

Recovery isn't what I imagined it to be, but I can promise you this: you will get through it—regardless of what addiction, trauma or struggle you are dealing with. You will heal.

Healing from my eating disorder, trauma, and mental health struggles taught me that the voices in my head convincing me to use destructive behaviors were not 100% me. I was being my own worst enemy because these voices had been programmed into me since childhood.

The staff at the Bella Vita really taught me that when I had a negative thought in my head, it stemmed from the negative core beliefs I had adopted as a child to fulfill my own needs at the time—as a result of a confusing, abusive, and traumatic childhood.

These are only a few negative core beliefs a person can have, but they are the ones I found most relatable. Negative core beliefs lead to negative self-talk and can drastically change your life. I know because they changed mine. I learned slowly through CBT (cognitive-based therapy) how to take steps to change these ways of thinking and beliefs about myself that weren't true.

I. Black and White Thinking (All or Nothing)

I used to think everything was 0% or 100% and that there wasn't a gray area. I was either recovered or hopeless. I was either accepted or hated. Black and white thinking for me was toxic because it didn't let me see the possibilities that things might be different.

II. Catastrophizing

When I was catastrophizing every situation in my life, it created more problems for me that dug me into a deeper hole of negative thinking. When I messed up in treatment and wasn't the perfect patient, I used this cognitive distortion. I told myself that because I failed at being the perfect patient, I was never going to recover and that I wasn't good enough to recover. This was not true.

III. Emotional Reasoning

Whenever I had a gut feeling about something negative, I was adamant about feeling that way, even if the universe gave me evidence counteracting it. For example, because I felt like I couldn't trust anyone and that the world was against me, no matter how much love or kindness people gave to me, I didn't think it was true. I was reasoning with my emotions that these people were being loving/caring/kind because they had bad intentions. Sometimes, our emotional reasoning convinces us and blindsides us to what is actually true. Speaking for myself, it was a mental filter that took everything from the world and filtered it so it matched my negative core belief. TEA.

IV. Self-Fulfilling Prophecy

Okay, so this one was mostly about self-sabotage for me. I would always predict that I would relapse and go back to my eating disorder, no matter how much help I got. So, when I planted that manifestation and energy into the universe, I acted on those behaviors, and it "confirmed" my predictions when I did go back to my eating disorder.

However, these predictions about yourself and the people around you can change. Slowly but surely, every time I thought of predictions/guesses that could confirm my negative beliefs about myself, I would list ten other possibilities to counteract it.

V. Personalizing (Self-Blame)

I was personally victimized by Dean Lin. No, but really though. I took everything to heart, and everything in my life that happened, I would blame myself. I always thought there was something inherently bad or negative about me, so I would take everything personally. Everyone's actions towards me I took personally. A good analogy I like to use when I find myself taking things personally is thinking about when I eat alone. I get insecure sometimes thinking everyone is watching me eat alone. But girl, in reality, everyone else is too focused on themselves; they don't reallygive a shit about you eating alone. OOP!

When other people are unkind or negative towards you, they are hurting and even dealing with their own traumas perhaps. They aren't targeting you specifically; they are just finding an outlet to project their issues the way they know how. As someone said before, hurt people *hurt* people...

VI. Shoulding On Yourself (Shitting On Yourself)

Have you met Dean, the king of shitting on himself and making it funny? Yeah, I still use comedy to this day to fix the "shoulding" in my life. However, I learned how to stop shoulding on myself so often because it affects my quality of life.

I used to "should" on myself for everything I did, making me spiral out of control with negative thinking. I would tell myself that I "should" do things like lose more weight, go to the gym, eat healthier, be more straight, etc. All this did was give me more anxiety and pressure to be at certain a mental state or position based on other people's expectations.

What negative core beliefs do you have?

List three and then list three thoughts counteracting that thought.

Negative Thought

_____
_____
_____
_____

Counteractive/Positive Thought

_____
_____
_____
_____

Negative Thought

_____
_____
_____
_____

Counteractive/Positive Thought

_____
_____
_____
_____

Negative Thought

_____
_____
_____
_____

Counteractive/Positive Thought

_____
_____
_____
_____

When I realized my eating disorder wasn't because of food, it was easier to separate my real self from my "disordered self." My eating disorder was the coping mechanism I learned as a way to deal with the hardships in life. Sometimes, you use destructive behaviors because that is the only way you know how to survive.

I was always beating myself up when I would relapse, but that was part of the problem: not being forgiving towards myself. Food was just a component of a more complicated structure, and I was able to finally see that I wasn't "dumb" or "afraid of food." It was simply because I didn't deal with the past that I had buried so deep.

People used to tell me, "Just eat!"

Girl, if it were that easy, you think I wouldn't have done it?

CHAPTER SEVENTEEN

Nourishing the Fabulous Trauma

Your past, negative life experiences, and your trauma do not make you a bad person. I know that is hard to believe because I believed that my past was my fault since I didn't deserve a "good life." However, traumas that made me who I am are events I would never take back.

I mean I obviously would not want to live through those traumas and negative life experiences again, but I am glad I went through what I went through. It has prepared me for other obstacles life could possibly throw at me in the future and it has made me the loving, compassionate, empathetic person I am today.

When I finally decided to LET GO, it was the first time I could actually see progress in my recovery and mental health. I was at war with myself for so long and wanted to stop reliving my past hurt every day.

IT'S WHAT HE DESERVES.

Letting go taught me so much about myself and my capabilities and gave me purpose to continue this arduous journey, aka life. When I let go, it wasn't pretty at all. Just imagine glitter but poorly placed glitter shaken onto the white glue you used in elementary school.

When I let go, treatment was harder than it ever was before. I had to feel the feelings I'd tried so hard to repress my entire life. When I let go, I did not erase the past. Instead, I stopped letting it affect my future. By acknowledging the trauma and feeding the abused child inside that I had never took the time to nourish, I discovered parts of my personality I never knew existed.

Starting treatment, everyone would tell me to "just eat." Bitch, it is not as simple as that. If it were that simple, then everyone could heal from "just" doing that thing to counteract their addiction! When I first started dealing with issues in rehab, I didn't know letting go was the key to starting the long journey of self-love.

I firmly believed that I was unlovable, and that in order for people to love me, I had to be PERFECT. Wrong. By prioritizing other people's happiness and by giving so much love to those around me, I felt empty. No matter how perfect of a patient I was, I realized that being perfect for others, trying to please others, and giving others what I don't give myself would only lead to my downfall.

The world, social media, and basically everything (ugh) convinces us that if we speak kindly to ourselves, we are failing. That is NOT TRUE! Our constant push for self-control and self-discipline is training us to hate ourselves more every day.

Our world feeds off our insecurities, so they feed us messages that become ingrained in us. Our healthcare prioritizes physical health and cuts mental health costs. And on top of that, we talk to ourselves like we aren't deserving of love, affection, or closeness.

I'm here to tell you that loving yourself isn't selfish. Loving yourself doesn't mean being conceited—gurl, don't get it confused. Loving yourself means loving yourself despite how you appear to the world, whether you conform to societal norms or not. Loving yourself means loving yourself even when you are sick, even when you are going through a rough time. It means acknowledging that even when things are hard, you are **CAPABLE** of love.

When you love yourself, you glow differently.

When you love yourself, you become open to possibilities beyond your wildest dreams.

When you love yourself, you allow others to love you back because you know you damn well deserve it. After all you went through? **GIRL**, you deserve it.

I want you to list six things you love about yourself. The catch is, they can't be physical. We body positive up in here, okay?

1. _____

_____

_____

_____

2. _____

_____

_____

_____

3. _____

_____

_____

_____

4. _____

_____

_____

_____

5. _____

_____

_____

_____

6. _____

_____

_____

_____

CHAPTER EIGHTEEN

That Shit Ain't Worth It

Because I was raised to associate abuse, negativity, and toxicity with love, I surrounded myself with relationships that reinforced all the self-sabotaging voices in my head. Unlearning this took time, and I still am unlearning parts of the negative voices in my head, even after years of therapy.

However, in my experience, when I learned to heal and detoxify the negative people in my life, I released energies that weren't serving me anymore. When I was constantly worrying about being judged by those I called "family" or "friends," I knew it was time to make a difference.

If you can identify these things in your life, then I challenge you to take steps in order to achieve the best life you deserve. Really sit down and think about the relationships in your life. Think about all of them, not just the positive ones, but also the ones that taught you lessons.

Which relationships fulfill you?

_____
_____
_____
_____

Which relationships make you feel drained?

_____
_____
_____
_____

What is your relationship with yourself? How do you want to maintain that relationship or change it if it is negative?

_____
_____
_____
_____
_____
_____
_____

Remember, don't take shit from anyone. But most importantly, stop treating yourself like shit. If you treat yourself like shit, you will accept the negative energy of people who conceal abuse as "love."

Okay, I know I've been sounding extremely preachy, but I learned this from someone who impacted my life while I was in treatment: Nurse Vanessa.

She was one of the only night time nurses that I connected with deeply during my third time in treatment. She gave me a whole new perspective on recovery that I hadn't even seen before. I think this is the lowkey tea to recovery: when the staff, other patients, and resources allow you different perspectives your negative thoughts didn't allow you to even consider.

I remember when Nurse Vanessa gave the patients and me the BIGGEST perspective change. She broke the rules for us, and part of me was confused but part of me was also excited. My eating disorder had waited for an escape for so long… except we weren't really escaping.

WE BROKE OUT OF TREATMENT!

No, just kidding. My eating disorder fucking wishes! She took us all to Denny's, and I was in shock because she was so different than the other nurses who treated us like patients who were below them. I know to the staff, we WERE patients, but at least treat us like people! It was nurses like Vanessa who proved statistics don't mean everything. She is a prime example of how taking a different approach can be life-saving.

Anyway, back to the Denny's story. I was nervous ALL night because I felt like we were breaking out of prison or something. She took us to Denny's and asked us to order whatever we wanted. But it was funny because all of us were still in recovery, so ordering out was still triggering and anxiety-provoking for us.

However, this exposure gave us so much courage in

recovery. I literally have a video of me eating ONE pecan and us all laughing over it. But the collective comedic moments of us making fun of our eating disorders may seem fucked up to the outside world, but for us who actually were going through this, it helped immensely.

For me, it helped me see that I did have issues and that I really needed to address them before they took more of my life away from me. Vanessa didn't coddle us like the other nurses or staff because she was blunt and told us how it was. The more I felt comfortable with her, the more I wanted to recover.

This is why to this day, I stan being triggered (in some cases). Being triggered taught me how to cope in a healthier way, instead of avoiding. Vanessa straight up told me I looked fucking SICK! And I know what you're thinking… WHAT?! No, but really. It may seem counterintuitive and might not work for everyone. However, for me, it did the opposite. Her free spirit, honesty and empathy came through as she was guiding me towards recovery.

"Honey, being sick ain't cute."

That quote stuck with me, as well as many quotes from my journal that I wrote down from our late nights. So, shout out to Vanessa. Thank you. Thank you with all my heart for teaching me how hard but beautiful it is to live. She taught me how to love myself even when I hated myself. She taught me how to laugh again, even through the immense pain I felt. She made me feel capable, loved, and nurtured. She acted like a loving mother to me, even when I was at my worst.

When I finally left residential treatment, I was scared. But with Vanessa's blessing and the promise I made myself to live a better life after treatment, I was ready.

After residential treatment, they didn't want me to go back to old behaviors whenever things got hard. I'm so grateful I listened and took things slower. Now I understand that no matter what, my health has to come first.

I was placed in a transitional living home before going back to school. It was a chance to prove to myself that I was strong enough to endure, accept, and let go of the pain my past had brought me; it was a chance for me to grow from it.

When they finally decided to discharge me from residential, I felt a sense of accomplishment. For the first time, I hadn't done something for others. It was selfish. I finally did something for myself. I deserved to be selfish because I had spent so much of my life trying to please others and the world around me.

Transitional living was hard—don't get me wrong. But transitional living taught me that coping skills ACTUALLY work when you truly want to be healthy or when you are in a place that you can choose the healthier, non-destructive behaviors.

There were days in transitional living when I thought I would go straight back into my eating disordered behaviors. But with constant group therapy, I felt like I was finally gaining control over my own life—this time without my eating disorder.

I didn't know how much of my old personality, life, and friendships were a direct result of my traumas, eating disorder, and mental health. The reason I was always so angry was because of all the pent-up pain and inability to have different perspectives to hard situations. I felt like a part of my brain had been freed from chains. I learned new things about myself, like what I really wanted in life and how I wanted to live my life on my own terms.

LIVING

CHAPTER NINETEEN

Fuck Dreams (That Aren't Your Dreams)

I officially discharged from treatment in October of 2016, but I still made sure I went to see a therapist. I was shocked at the progress I had made. I had completed something I never knew I could. I was in the body that made me feel the best. When I was "kinda" recovered, I would obsess about an ideal weight, but I learned that getting off a meal plan and accepting intuitive eating was the best thing anyone could do for themselves.

And NO, I'm not talking about intuitive eating like skipping breakfast and eating only clean foods. Actual intuitive eating, health, and peace of mind comes with not listening to the hunger cues from a disordered or diet-centric way, but from a nourishing mindset.

Finally, I let my body just breathe after years of trying to diet or manipulate my physical appearance for the world. Treating my body right, my body did me favors back. That's why I believe in giving what you want given back to you.

I didn't realize how long a day was until I gave up my behaviors, even if I spent some hours trying to cope and not fall back into old behaviors. But trust me, not acting on and trying to stop destructive behaviors is leaps above being IN the destruction.

The hours I would spend starving myself, purging, binge eating, and weighing myself had been freed to give me more time to think, reflect, practice self-care, and most importantly, be creative.

I had been trying to please my parents all my life, but after realizing I had to live for myself, I found new passions and career paths that I enjoyed working in. This is when I decided that learning anything STEM (science, technology, engineering and math) related was not in my future. It wasn't something I wanted to continue investing my time in because quite frankly, it didn't make me happy. Although I spent years learning about aviation, trying to be the perfect student, it was time I opened my heart and embraced the creative, outgoing and FABULOUS person I was meant to be.

Before treatment, I thought I had to be in a career that stressed me out but made my parents happy. But now thinking back, why? At the end of the day, I realized that although my parents did raise me and give me life, shouldn't MY happiness matter?

When I was discharged from treatment several months later, I switched my major from kinesiology to film/media (my school liked to call it media, arts and culture), but I guess that's a liberal arts education.

I remember listening to stories from those around me who were well into careers that didn't fulfill them. This scared me. It scared me because with all that I had gone through, I didn't deserve a future that didn't fulfill me. It's never too late to realize your passions.

I didn't want to look back on life and think, "What if?" I wanted to live fearlessly and to live life unapologetically, for myself.

After I reached this epiphany and realization, I knew this choice would be one that changed my life trajectory. Dare I say, it was the biggest epiphany in my life?

Okay fine, minus the time I realized I was gay.

I knew that being a kinesiology major was NOT in my best interest. First of all, I didn't enjoy doing it, and I always felt like I was being forced into doing it. Second of all, it was triggering AF because it made me obsess even more about my body and nutrition. I majored in it only to please not only my parents but also my eating disorder. We LOVE a self-analyzing queen.

I made a promise to myself and wrote it down. I promised myself that I would be more than my eating disorder and my mental battles, and I would make an impact on the world. The fact that I didn't see much Asian representation in Hollywood growing up pushed me to work harder and continue to hustle my way to the top.

No more negative energy. No more making my life about pleasing other people and getting their acceptance. As long as I accepted myself, no one's judgement mattered.

Through therapy, I slowly accepted myself, and before I knew it... I had learned that accepting, loving, and caring for myself was the only way out and the thing I NEEDED in this world to become whole.

CHAPTER TWENTY

Rejections Are the Best

When I discovered my new passion for entertainment, I had zero relevant experience that would qualify me for any entertainment-related internship. The only things on my resume were from Bed, Bath & Beyond, a sushi restaurant, and an on-campus job.

At this point, I was still in a program called the Opportunity Network, which I probably forgot to mention earlier. But I was in it from my sophomore year of high school until the end of college. They knew how messy I was career-wise because I was too scared to share any personal struggles until later on.

Something that I don't really find productive is when people tell teenagers they are indecisive or aloof for showing interest in multiple careers. Girl, let people discover their passions! I kept shifting from different career paths. At first, I wanted to act (but realized there wasn't any diversity in Hollywood at the time, tea), then I wanted to do STEM (for my parents, never again), and I ultimately landed on wanting to be in entertainment again.

See? A MESS.

However, I will say that everything I found uninteresting taught me what I am passionate about.

When I received an email from one of the staff at the Opportunity Network about media internships, I was reading through all the job descriptions worrying about my qualifications. But I decided to send my resume anyway and apply to internships in ANY—I mean literally ANY—entertainment-related internship.

And you know the tea behind my fear of rejection and people not accepting me, so this was particularly anxiety inducing for me. I remember getting emails everyday thinking that I was going to get at least ONE interview from the twenty internships I had applied to.

I got no responses from anyone and was discouraged.... However, I used the coping skills they taught me in treatment to use my wise mind and to not take things personally to the point I affected my mental health. Just because you are getting no's doesn't mean you are untalented or unwanted. It just means you are being redirected. Sometimes, you'll get the spins from being "redirected" so many times, but an opportunity will fall into place.

I told myself that this summer, even without an internship, I would do something creative on my own. Suddenly, on one random day in March of 2017, I received a call really early before class. I had gotten a call from somewhere I didn't even apply to. Turns out, the recruiter forwarded my resume that I used to apply to other internships within the company.

I was shaking.

It was a call from *The Daily Show with Trevor Noah*!

Okay, at this point, I thought someone was prank calling

me because I was seriously confused. First, I hadn't applied and secondly, they wanted to set an interview up to talk to the hiring managers. WELL, turns out it was not a prank call, and I ended up getting interviewed by Jessie and Lisa. These two amazing people not only sparked the start of my career in entertainment, but they also taught me everything I needed to know in the industry to persevere.

If you're reading this, I AM GRATEFUL!

This shifted my mindset about getting no's for an answer. Almost all the time, no's lead you ultimately to where you're meant to be. When someone finally says yes, like Jessie and Lisa said yes to me, that is ALL that matters. All the no's teach you to work harder, to be stronger, and to believe in yourself until someone says yes. This yes turned out to be a place where I met so many other interns like Sara, one of the greatest people I know, and also Elise, Stacey, Christina, and so many more.

A lot of the time, social media and our world try to hide the failures, but I think embracing failures helped me immensely. It made my experiences real, unedited, and STILL GLITTERY. I try to tell everyone that just because I got this one opportunity, doesn't mean my dad knew the CEO of a company. TEA. This one opportunity didn't make me better than anyone; it was simply after an abundance of no's that someone said yes because I had said yes to myself.

It didn't matter if no one chose me, because I knew as long as I chose me, I would be okay.

What ways have you been rejected, and how will you choose yourself every single day despite the pressure from the world?

_____

_____

_____

_____

_____

_____

_____

_____

_____

_____

_____

From *The Daily Show*, I moved onto Paramount Pictures with the blessing of the recruiter, Essence, who introduced me to the recruiter in Los Angeles (Jed and Xhana).

I know I said earlier about not letting no's get to you, but every time I apply for a new opportunity, I always have to remind myself that it is okay to feel let down or disappointed. My golden rule is to allow myself to feel my feelings, to be upset about it and to get it off my chest for a few hours, MAX. Then I'm back to being a boss-ass bitch not giving a fuck.

Ok, just kidding about the not giving a fuck part, but you get what I mean. You could think of it as "going back to being the fabulous person you ALWAYS are." There, a PG-13 version.

Anyway, I wasn't 100% qualified for the diversity and inclusion position at Paramount but again, you'd be surprised at the possibility that some Hollywood executives ACTUALLY want to help you. In this case, Anita and Meaghan believed in me, even though I really thought I had bombed my interview. I'm dramatic, but it was really bad. I was convinced that I wouldn't get the position, but unexpectedly, even after all the no's from other companies, I stayed hopeful and got a YES from them.

Every time you think you're finished learning, you're not. And if you are in an environment where you're not learning, then in my experience, it's time to move on. Know yourself enough and know your worth. Anita and Meaghan taught me so many things I didn't even think I needed to know. The trust, time, and effort they put into me restored a lot of my faith in the industry that everyone had told me was harsh, cruel and unattainable. Others in the office, like Adrian, Debbie, Franchesca, Joya, and Helen, made it all feel like a complete family. Anita went from being just a "boss" to what I like to call my Mom 2.0. If you're reading this, you're still listed on my phone as Mom 2.0.—you can't get rid of me just YET! HA.

As I was saying, she became Mom 2.0 to me because she trained me to take constructive criticism with the best attitude, to see things from a different perspective, and to maintain empathy, love, and compassion for others even when people were being negative or rude.

I remember when I would feel lonely at school because I was juggling classes, therapy, and trying so hard to maintain my recovery. But whenever I knew I had to come into the office, I felt a sense of joy, no matter what my mood was.

You might think my life was perfect at this point, but I will tell you that I am not perfect and wasn't perfect then. There's something beautiful about being imperfect because you get to live a life of experience, liveliness and spontaneity. I've had my hard days with my eating disorder, worrying, my career, school, and friendships. But above all, I had people who supported me because I was vulnerable to them, I let them in. I let Anita and Meaghan in, and I don't regret being vulnerable. They saw the ugly sides of me and still treated me with kindness.

I was an anxious mess towards the end of my internship with Paramount because they had a limit to how many semesters/hours you could intern. I didn't want to leave the family I had gotten so close to, but Mom 2.0 told me that I needed to leave to learn more about myself. I got another plethora of no's until I got a yes to one of the biggest opportunities I could have imagined; I did not expect to get this yes at all. I kept worrying, but Anita introduced me to Niti, who helped me get the one yes into the Academy Gold Program.

See a pattern here? I got so many no's from opportunities I don't even think about today. What does matter is realizing the no's in my life shaped my career path to what it is today. I remember in a TV show, a mother said to her daughter that she was one heartbreak away from a happily ever after. I kind of use that analogy for my career. Every no brought me closer to that one yes I didn't know would bless my life.

What no's have you gotten and what are some yes's you've gotten? Write them down so you can come back to them when you feel like a no is really affecting you. Remind yourself of your greatness!

_____
_____
_____
_____
_____
_____
_____
_____
_____
_____
_____

In Academy Gold, I got to meet amazing people from the staff, to interns, to industry professionals, and I learned so much I couldn't learn from school. Slight drag at my school, but like everyone has opinions, right? I also feel that life experiences always teach you more than the education system.

From feeling like Hollywood executives were so far from reach, they suddenly became real people to me. Their stories inspired me because similarly, everyone gets no's in their life. More often than not, it's always about that one YES that propels you forward.

I always think about how different my life would be if another opportunity had said yes to me. The people I have come to love, the things I have learned about myself, and the person I have become would ALL be different.

After Academy Gold, I still wanted to be behind the camera and work in film. However, when I was interviewed for a production company after applying on CBS's website, my life changed without me even knowing it yet. Starting my internships off on the TV side of entertainment and finding my way back to TV—I mean, full circle.

Fulwell 73–it was an unexpected blessing I didn't even know was coming. I knew it when Kevin, the unscripted development producer, was fine with me interviewing right as I WAS HOPPING out of the shower with a popped eye vessel. HAHA!

No, but seriously. I felt comfortable being myself immediately after starting at Fulwell. This was my last internship before graduation, and I'd grown throughout the years in college while keeping an open mind. I worked with Katharine/KB/Sister, Kevin, Rheanna, Jeff, Meredith, Emma, Tracie, Katherine, Brett and Jill. Jill and I were both interns and Fulwell became family because I saw how they treated one another, how they lifted each other up, and how much they wanted to help me learn more about myself.

KB, Kevin, and everyone at Fulwell trusted Jill and me with so much that it made me feel like my voice mattered in this industry, even as a gay, person of color who had come from a dark past. I know what it's like to be someone else, in the closet and ingenuine. However, with them, I didn't feel like I needed to have my walls up. They made me love parts of myself I didn't think I could love. Before them, I used to think my "obnoxious," fun and quirky personality could be too much and I had to tone it down. Unconsciously, by being around positivity and people who lifted each other up every day, I became the best unapologetic version of myself.

CHAPTER TWENTY-ONE

Strut, Step, and Glitter

You are never promised tomorrow, so live today. Ew, did that literally just come out of my mouth? SOUNDS cliché, but it is very true. After almost dying from an eating disorder, I could not worry about the future anymore. I had to focus on what I had in front of me and practice mindfulness and being present. Loving in the moment. Laughing in the moment.

Worrying about the opinions of others will cause a cycle of pain and suffering that will not end—I learned that the hard way. Girl, if anyone tries to judge you, tries to take away your self-love, and is overall a negative energy in your life, I'm here to tell you that it has nothing to do with your inner core as a person. Remember that everyone is projecting, and people's worlds usually revolve around themselves.

Be yourself no matter what anyone else thinks of you. We are on borrowed time. The death of Kobe Bryant and his daughter Gianna gave me a recent mental awakening to what I am iterating. If you think about it, nothing really matters (not even the tea) other than how much love you give to those around you, how you treat those around you, how you impact others and how much you love yourself.

Throughout the trauma, recovery, and my experience, I used comedy as a way of "free therapy." Similar to a sibling relationship, I can make fun of myself, but if someone else tries to joke about my struggles—girl, are we going to fight or what?

Like I said earlier, laughing when you're in pain is powerful. Knowing and making my trauma and struggles into a "comedic moment" was cathartic for me—it put the issues outside of myself. This made me realize that I was always deserving of happiness, no matter what the world told me, and I want you to know the same. YOU, whoever you are, deserve the best life has to offer.

How are you going to stop worrying about your future and your eyebrows? I'm only kidding.

How are you going to change vicious cycles that aren't moving you towards a life you want? What things in your life will you change in order to manifest and be truly "living your best life" for yourself and not for the internet or anyone else?

_____

_____

_____

_____

_____

_____

What is your strut, step, and glitter?

CHAPTER TWENTY-TWO

Going for It (And Being Fabulous All the Way)

Listen, I know from experience that going for it is hard, especially when you have past baggage, trauma, or mental health struggles, like I did. Through all the pain and going through recovery, I still had to be persistent.

I went for it even after I found out I was diagnosed with dysthymia, also known as persistent depressive disorder, which was different from my previous diagnosis of just being depressed. Coupled with dysthymia, I was dealing with ADHD and anxious distress. Honestly, I don't even know how they decided on it, but I know I went through a longer process this time to get diagnosed and to make sure I was being diagnosed properly.

If that ain't enough, the psychiatrist said I also was dealing with some type of personality disorder. Despite all this, I didn't let stigma or this diagnosis paralyze or control my life.

Girl, don't get me wrong. I was devastated and was anxious about suddenly getting all these "diagnoses," which I don't even like to call them. I like to talk about everyone's uniqueness and how they experience the world. Now, how did I get over this and not turn back to destructive behaviors to numb them out?

I was realizing now that I have a uniqueness to me that might mean I have to work harder to "function" in a society that stigmatizes mental health. That made me a mental health advocate and want to fight to de-stigmatize the way we talk about it. My diagnosis was on paper, and with fresher eyes after feeling the feelings of anxiety, acceptance, and acknowledgement, I saw it from a more objective perspective.

Looking at the things I've struggled with, I was able to write things down and slowly work on improving the little parts of myself. I wanted to stay accountable to myself, ensuring I was living my best life and ensuring the relationships I tried hard to cultivate were going in the direction I wanted. No more bullshit and no more projecting negative core beliefs onto myself and on the relationships I value most in my life.

Instead of being SAD, it is time to be G(AY)LAD!

Okay, you might think, "Dean, WTF?! I thought you said to feel your feelings."

YES, I did say feel your feelings. I want you to feel all the pain, sadness, and trauma. You can let the sadness out, cry, and be horizontal in bed. However, I want you to be GLAD after the fact. GLAD because you WILL let the sadness leave. You won't let the sadness inside you stay there and create another negative voice in your mind. You won't let it rob you of any happiness.

In my life, and in all our lives actually, we are surrounded by negative energy and people projecting their own sadness, pain, and trauma onto others because they've never dealt with it. When you start thinking like this, you can let sadness go and be glad again.

Nothing is REALLY about you when others lash out.

Anyway, back to my brand. The fact is, we are surrounded by diet culture, there is no doubt about that. We can't even use the word *healthy* without ruining it. This is why we can't have nice things… When people say healthy, they're most likely trying to fit societal ideals and getting tricked by diet culture, saying intuitive eating and intermittent fasting is "healthy." Like girl, the diet industry is so creative, they made another name for skipping breakfast. Oop.

Working in Hollywood, I have become used to the sayings that would trigger my eating disorder in the past. Everyone says, "Oh, it's just the industry." However, I'm here to tell you that it is in FACT the industry, but that does not mean you can't be the change that can inspire others to stop talking negatively towards themselves.

So many coworkers and people I've talked to throughout my life, Los Angeles included (ESPECIALLY L.A.), feel SO bad about overeating, when it does not make you a bad person when you indulge!

A common one, "I shouldn't have eaten seven cookies," or "I need to be good today and not eat that (foods society deems as unhealthy)."

Girl, stop letting food control you like that. I let food control me in that way for almost my whole life, I don't want you to get stuck in a cycle where you equate what you put into your body as part of your self-worth.

Whenever I hear these things, I feel a bit angry. Not at the person, but I think at the way society has conditioned us to be insecure about every little thing. Maybe if ads, diet trends, and fitness experts stopped telling people to restrict and count their calories, they wouldn't be in a cycle of restriction and then binge eating?

IDK, HUN, JUST A THOUGHT.

But no really, I hear it every single day: in entertainment, on the street, in grocery stores, EVERYWHERE. The diet industry is one of the biggest industries that is making us feel more insecure about ourselves because they always promise that the key to happiness is weight loss.

Wrong. I can confidently say that losing weight initially made me feel euphoric; starving myself felt euphoric, and it made others accept me, but that is not a reason to lose weight. It did not make me happier. It made me angry all the time, and no matter how much weight I lost, it wasn't enough. If I was losing weight, I was happy for a second, but the more weight I lost, the more depressed and anxious I was around people/food/social interactions.

To avoid this, I want you to live your life in balance, reevaluating the word *health* and making the best choices for YOUR life. Reclaim the word health and don't let the diet industry convince you that dieting is the only way to be "healthy."

Don't let the world take you away from your donuts (partly kidding), but seriously, don't let the world teach you that eliminating a whole food group is the only way to be healthy and good. This cycle of dieting gave me illusions of health and of feeling "good" because it made me feel like I belonged, but do you really want to belong in a society where everyone is insecure? Where everyone's insecurities are being taken advantage of by capitalism?

Rethinking the way we relate to our bodies is extremely important. Remember, queens, these bodies are meant to take care of us, and at the end of the day, it is about how much we show our love, how much love we spread, and the meaningful relationships we cultivate in this lifetime.

Our bodies are all different and can be healthy at any size, because we were born unique. We all have different genetic make-ups, different life experiences, and different lifestyles that should not be a copy of others.

At the end of the day, you were born to stand out, to be different.

Your uniqueness is yours alone, and after going through everything I have gone through, I realize the importance of reclaiming my difference and making it my own. Because being different isn't so bad after all. Being different helped me shine in ways beyond my imagination. Instead of going through life, I'm learning to live it.

What cycles of dieting have you gone through, and what steps do you want to take to stop?

_____
_____
_____
_____
_____

What meaningful relationships in your life can you rely on to help you on this path to self-love?

_____
_____
_____
_____
_____

What steps will you take to stop feeling like you are "bad" because you ate food not deemed "healthy" by society's definition? Be real with yourself.

_____

_____

_____

_____

List all the diets you will **NOT** be trying this year, and try to stay away from them. I want you to remember a time when you felt extremely "bad" about your body and write it down. Close your eyes and bring yourself back to that moment and tell that person they are good, they are okay, and these feelings are temporary—they served their purpose.

_____

_____

_____

_____

_____

_____

_____

_____

It is time to let go.

CHAPTER TWENTY-THREE

Not for Fame, Not for Clout

Queens, it's sad to be finishing this book, but I want you to know that I wrote this not only for you, but also for me. Like I've said earlier, I'm not perfect by any means, but that didn't mean I couldn't write a book to help others. Don't get me wrong, I didn't write this book for fame, and I want you to know that although our world is filled with desire to stand out and to be out of the ordinary…fame isn't the answer.

I mean, it would be great to be famous (because let's be real, I LOVE attention). Haha. But no, I've found my voice through vulnerability, writing and doing what I love. I know the fame will come, but I genuinely am not doing it because of the popularity. I've tried the vanity/popularity mindset and tried going that route. CLEARLY, it did not work for me.

My mindset going into the industry and into my future

involves seeing fame and popularity as a way to help spread a message that will change the world. I want to use my platform to help those struggling with trauma, eating disorders, and whatever else is going on inside of them, causing them to suffer.

From wanting to be white, to actually loving myself—the Asianness, my brown eyes, and ALL I have to offer to this world--I realized I don't want to do it for fame. It will come and will help me financially, yes, but not focusing on the materialistic version of it has freed me immensely.

I think fame is a double-edged sword, and I want to dull the side that makes you change into a worse version of yourself. In my case, fame will be a platform used for the greater good.

However, fame and finances will come through manifestation—I know it. But if it doesn't, that is also okay because life is more than that. Life is about wanting more but also leaving your own legacy, even if it's just to those around you. I know that after healing from my struggles, every little impact I make in this world can still be considered positive change. That is ENOUGH and that is OKAY.

Knowing this has helped inspire me to host my own talk show in the future, and it has given me motivation to take action on all the wonderful passions I've had my whole life. Changing the world starts with baby steps, and I'd hope that my podcast (Pretty Gaysic with Dean Lin), my TEDx talk on negative self-talk, and this book has given you hope.

Having a platform that I created, no matter how small, reminds me of those who have reached out because of my story and struggles. Those who said I've inspired or helped them seek treatment, makes this all worth it.

In times of difficulty, I remember those moments and propel myself forward. Sharing my vulnerable side has been hard all my life, but I know this way of living makes me more real, raw, and genuine.

To this day, I have to catch myself every time I touch my own body. I have to make a conscious choice not to body check. I have to consciously put in effort every single day to not let my past catch up to my future and affect the life I want to live. I don't want you to finish this book and go away thinking I am better than you, more capabable than you. I am not.

I am not perfect, but I will use my platform to help those of you who feel alone and unloved to feel joy and love, and to laugh along with me. All the while, I will teach you all that loving yourself is so important, even if the world tries to convince you that being hard on yourself is the only way to succeed.

The world can convince you that if you're a person of color, a woman, LGBTQ+, don't conform or are anything other than the mainstream, you don't belong.

Don't give them that power, YOUR power. You are in control and have power in your life, even if it may not feel that way. I want you to repeat that every single day. You are worth it no matter the ups and downs that happen in life.

Remember, queens, the best thing about struggle and happiness is that *nothing lasts forever*. That is the best and scariest quote. It means that nothing bad (the pain, trauma, etc.) does not last forever so you will get out of it. It also means that nothing good lasts forever, so learn to cherish the good things and be present in the moment, living your life like there is no tomorrow. Because literally, it isn't promised.

Life is so unpredictable, but you have a friend in me, duh! You don't always have to get it right with me or even get it right in general. You have permission to be yourself. Always. You and I—we both won't get it right all the time, but at the end of the day, the things we struggle with and don't get right will be the very things that guide us to the top.

Remember that when damaged, insecure, and hurt people talk about you, it's because they can't be vulnerable and talk about themselves. They're afraid that when they talk about themselves, no one will listen. Ouch, did you get burned by that tea? Some got on me and it's stung.

After you start throwing away negative energies in your life that cause you stress, you will gain mental clarity, hence feeling all your feelings but not letting them have power over your life's trajectory. Remember, every time you want to say something negative about yourself, pretend that you are talking to a child or to your best friend. Would you say that to them? 'Cause if you would not say it to them, girl, you best not be saying it to yourself.

I'd like to end with a science lesson. Okay, just kidding, not really. But remember when Newton said energy is not created nor destroyed? The loving, kind, and empathetic energy you put out, you must give and keep to yourself sometimes. Energy is transferred, but you can't forget about yourself. Remember to find a balance where you can be a boss-ass bitch who is **FABULOUS** and loving to others while showing yourself the same respect.

Write your mission statement and life vision. It can't include anything physical that you want to "fix" or anything you will have to change yourself for (unless it is a destructive behavior/negative energy you want to change).

_____
_____
_____
_____
_____
_____
_____
_____
_____
_____
_____
_____
_____
_____
_____
_____
_____
_____
_____
_____
_____
_____
_____

DEAN LIN

CHAPTER TWENTY-FOUR

A Love Letter to You

Thank you so much for reading *Dean's Way Out*. I feel like I have grown so much writing this book, as I got to reexperience everything in my life. Granted, this isn't my life in full detail, but you stuck around anyway.

As some of you may know me from childhood, high school, college, work and even my podcast, I want to thank you. I want to thank everyone who has been part of my journey to healing and to finding myself. I wouldn't be here if it weren't for the lessons you've all taught me.

There were details that I wanted to include in this book but didn't because you'd be here forever. No, I'm totally kidding. I wanted this book to be as therapeutic for you as it was for me. I wanted you to laugh but also to gain something valuable from it. This book allowed me to open up to the world and to share my story, giving my childhood and past its well-deserved recognition but also giving me closure.

I know I talk a lot about how the negative things in my life propelled me forward, but I also hope that kids growing up don't need to deal with all these traumas in order to live happily. I hope children growing up—with proper and positive guidance—can live their life and have their needs fulfilled, starting the day they were born.

I talk a lot about how shitty my parents and my family life were, but I also want you to know that I have forgiven, but I have not forgotten the trauma. I spent a long time blaming them, but I found peace writing this book, and I found peace in accepting that all the things wrong in my life gave me the most valuable life lessons.

My family life was hard, but my parents did help me grow into the person I am today, and without them, I would not exist, so for that I am eternally grateful. I know deep down they tried to raise me the best they could, with what they knew and with how **THEY** were raised.

I see it all the time with my grandmother. Whenever she nurtured me and took great care of me, I saw it in her eyes that she wanted to make up for raising my mother the wrong way. And by wrong way, I mean teaching her styles of communication that passed on generationally.

However, I vow to myself that I won't pass on a tradition of gaslighting or negative parenting—when I become one myself, of course.

I hope the growth I made throughout my life can help you continue your growth and blossoming. I hope you realize that you don't have to experience life the way you were taught (if it isn't the life you want).

I want you to know that whoever you are, it is okay. I don't ever want you to attach yourself or your self-worth to a diet, a person, a company, a place, or a project. I want you to attach yourself to your own purpose, your own dreams, and your own vision so you can be as powerful as you want to be.

The last thing I want to tell you is:

I want you to forgive the wrongdoings and trauma you've faced in your life so you can be peaceful, but also so you can move on and not hold on to any lingering feelings that won't serve you positively.

I want you to put yourself first, no matter what others think of you. The most important relationship in life is the relationship you have with yourself.

I want you to love the person you are becoming like tomorrow isn't promised.

I want you to live your happiest life and not settling for less than you deserve. Granted, there will be bad days, but you will get through them.

I want you to believe in yourself, even when no one else believes in you.

I want you to feel whole and to realize that everything else in your life is an addition to the masterpiece you already are.

I am still figuring out my own life, but trust me, it will always work out. It will always work out because when you acknowledge the wise and positive parts of your brain, and when you differentiate the voices of your traumas that mislead your life, only good can happen.

One of my favorite things that Oprah said in an interview before she got famous was this:

"I will do well because I'm not defined by a show. I think we are defined by the way we treat ourselves and the way we treat other people. It would be wonderful to be acclaimed as this talk show host who made it—that would be wonderful! But if that doesn't happen, there are other important things in my life."

This interview of hers has inspired me to not do it for the fame, but also to recreate the definition of what I see as successful in my life. As long as I have loved as much as I could towards others, including myself, and have people in my life who care about me, I've made it.

Repeat after me: I am so beautiful, in all the ways possible. The love, empathy, and my existence offers so much that you can't place a price tag on it. My energy, aura and laughter is infectious. I radiate so much positive energy, love, happiness, healing, blessing, peace, and life. I can and will always be my own savior, soulmate, best friend, and inspiration. I believe in myself and choose myself even when no one else does. I love myself unconditionally—always.

Love,
Dean from Queens

ACKNOWLEDGMENTS

A dreamer by the name of Brian D. Johnson inspired me to bring this book into the world. Thank you, words cannot describe how grateful I am for you. You have given me the courage to experience, manifest, and live my life to the fullest. The world sees you as a dreamer, inspirational speaker, and host. I am so lucky to know how vulnerable, giving, and reliable you are. You are a close friend, mentor, and big brother I needed to guide me throughout my journey to becoming.

Cindy Lin is the strongest and best sister in the world. She is the reason why I made it through my childhood alive. Without you, I wouldn't be able to recognize the gaslighting we have grown up enduring. Cindy, if you hadn't been the sister to a bratty, in the closet, and obnoxious little brother, I don't know who I would be. You are more than a sister to me, you are my only supportive family, and you are home. I love you more than I can ever describe in words. I am so lucky to have you in my life, reminding me that I will never be alone regardless if I feel lonely. I am forever grateful.

An amazing woman by the name of Micaela D. Stevens changed my perspectives on friendships, love, and belonging. I still can't believe how much we've gone through together, and I hope we share our iPhone locations until we're old. You are someone I can count on, always. We don't need to say a single word to one other to understand what the other is feeling and thinking. I think that is a testament to how strong our bond is. Thank you for loving me despite all my flaws, through treatment, and all the bad days.

The people who gave me my life back, thank you to the Bella Vita, Luci Masredjian, Matt Calkins, and Vanessa Marrero. Vanessa, thank you for teaching me how to live. Here's to those who went through treatment with me and taught me lessons throughout my journey– Amy, Morgan, Matea, Cassie, Maria, Shari, and more. Without you all, I might not be writing this book or even on this earth. You have my word that I will live for myself. Your constant support and guidance helped me get into treatment, heal, and live my life the way I wanted. You helped spark the desire in me to take care of myself and help others do the same.

Thank you to everyone at The Opportunity Network for always being so supportive of me during high school and college. You all were a blessing in my life–Ray Reyes, Emmanuel Moses, AiLun Ku, Jessica Pliska, Eric Santiago, Megan Nestor, James Nadeau, and more. Along with people in the program that I call good friends even after six years and me moving away–Scarlyn Cuevas, Daniela Charris, Daniela Carela, Yoksaidy Sutil, Sachiko, and more.

To the people who kept me sane in high school–Marizeli Diaz, Jennifer Ludizaca, Farha Faruk, Cesar Nunez, Chris Sperrazza,

Amira Hamirani and the teachers at Aviation that guided me through. I was dealing with my issues, but you all were there for me even when I did not feel at home within myself. Marizeli, from the bottom of my heart, I am blessed to know you. You didn't judge me from the moment we met in Engineering class, and even though I was dealing with shit inside, I hope you know you were a light in my life. Thank you to Aviation High School for throwing hardships at me and challenging me. Without it, I might still be in the closet and living at home.

I want to send love to all my gays at Occidental College, yellow 3, and people who have been there since day one. The ones that have been there for me, even at my worst, thank you for not canceling me and giving me second chances after I was in a mentally better place.

You all made me feel like it was impossible to leave Occidental. I vowed to myself that I wouldn't miss college because of the struggles I went through. But you all changed my perspective. I miss and love you: Adriana, Anneke, Anabel, Mak, Olivia, Molly, Ella, Maggie, Nina, Teagan, Dion, Beau, and Matt. And of course, Lauren Parks and Lauren Long, I love you both and I'm so happy we became such good friends.

Aria Bryan, Esme Brown, Megan Chichester, Theresa Edwards, Lindsey Ingram, Clark Leazier, Lily Moffet, Phoebe Patterson, and Dej Williams. Thank you for being in my life. To the ones in my major that made the last year of college worth it. Taylor, Raphael, Alex, Cherry, Carolynn, Alia, Lars, Nasira, and to my professors.

Thank you, Essence Dashtaray, for making it possible for my resume to land on Jessie Kanevsky and Lisa Cortez's desk. Thanks for believing in me and opening the door for me into the entertainment industry. To everyone at The Daily Show, thank you for teaching me so much. Elise Terrell, Stacey Angeles,

Kaitlin Alm, Amir Combs, Christina Pelletiere, and all the talented people I was able to work alongside.

Sara Essa, another intern I worked with that I love dearly. I'll never forget the D'Agostino runs. I think I have the aisles memorized still. I can't wait to see where our friendship takes us. We're far in distance, but close by heart. You are a special friend.

Thank you, Jed Saba and Xhana Numpang, for helping me navigate my journey into Paramount Pictures. I got to meet Anita Ortiz, Meaghan Devine, Debbie Benami-Rahm, Franchesca Ramirez, Adrian Auld, Joya McCrory, and more. Anita and Meaghan, thank you for being two amazing people that entered my life. You are a blessing, taught me valuable lessons and kept me grounded every day. Anita, my mom 2.0., thank you for teaching me that my talents are worth it and that I am worth it, even when this industry can be harsh. When I vented to you about my struggles, you accepted me with open arms and never judged me.

Of course, I'd like to thank the Academy of Motion Picture Arts and Sciences. Niti Shah, who vouched for me and allowed me to be part of the program. The staff at the Academy, Randy, Bettina, Angelle, Erica, Tracy, and more. Everyone who participated in the program as interns. You all taught me so much about myself.

Claudia Juarez and Rachel Kipp, thanks for being obnoxious with me (only partly kidding). Y'all are two of the funniest and kindest people I know–always knowing the right things to say to make me laugh, feel better, and I love who I am around y'all.

Fulwell 73–Katharine Bremner, Jeff Grosvenor, Kevin Joseph, Meredith Fox, Rheanna Sorenson, Emma Conway, Tracie Fiss, Brett Blakeney, Katherine Blidy, Amanda Ahmad, and Tayo Amos. Thank you for letting me be myself, helping me figure out my passions, and supporting me in everything I do.

KB and Kevin, thank you for giving the opportunity to learn as an intern. Meredith, thank you for always making sure I was taken care of, and for helping me navigate adulthood into a full-time job. Jeff, your work ethic and hustle inspire me to achieve my dreams. Your free-spirit, grit, support, and kindness motivates me.

Katharine Bremner, we went from co-workers to friends, to family. You are my sister away from home and my rock. Without your constant love and support, I might not know some positive parts of me that I bring into this world. I can't wait to see where the future takes us. You inspire me every single day and seeing you brightens up my darkest days. You never make me feel like a burden, but most importantly, you never judge me—instead, you support me every step of the way.

Rheanna, thank you for the endless positivity and love. Our friendship makes me smile and I can't wait to sip tea (actually mimosas) on vacation, laughing about the times we didn't know if we would make it.

Emma, thank you for always challenging me, and pushing me to think harder, be more creative and come up with things I never knew I could ideate.

Lexa Payne shot the cover of this book. You are so talented and one of the most giving, caring and nurturing women I know. I am so lucky we unexpectedly crossed paths, and I'm so excited to see what else you accomplish. You make me trust friendship and let my walls down.

Maricela Naranjo, you made me believe in roommates again. You opened your arms to me when I moved in, and I couldn't be more grateful. I used to fear going home and would get anxious about having roommates because of my past roommate horror stories. But now, having you in my life has made a living situation a home. I can always be myself around you, regardless of what

I'm going through. You are honest, you are kind, and you are my family. I love you, Cela. I can't believe we both manifested for better roommates and found each other. I can't wait to share our obsession with grapes wherever life takes us.

Tyler-Anne Crosby, also known as t.a.c.o, you bring the adventure out in me. Thank you for always going on last minute trips with me, taking my Santa Barbara virginity, and showing me one of the best seafood restaurants on the coast. I don't remember exactly how we became such close friends, but I'm so glad I found you. You're a gem, and you make me smile.

Carpool Karaoke staff, thank you for teaching me so much during season three. Andrew Zilch and Taya Faber, thank you for always rooting for me, being goofy with me, and inspiring me to do better for myself, even when I don't feel good mentally. Eric, the writers, production and post-production team, thank you for allowing me to jump on board this well oiled machine, and helped me learn as much as I can.–accepting my dramatic, extroverted and overall persona.

Michael Broun, Casey Stewart, Pattie Lin, Kathryn Hammond, Bradford Wilson, Lou Trabbie, and Sydney Stanford–thanks for being good friends and for many wholesome memories. Bradford, Sydney, and Kathryn, y'all see me at my worst, and by worst I mean 6AM in the gym. So much love for you all. Pattie, thank you for encouraging me to stay accountable and I love that we have the same last names. What screams family more than that?

... And to you reading this book. Thank you for giving me your time and allowing me to be vulnerable. I hope you laughed, related, and took something away from this book.

Over & Out

xx

ABOUT THE AUTHOR

Dean Lin has overcome many personal challenges, including eating disorders, depression, and being in the closet. Dean grew up in Queens, New York. Dean is a #1 Amazon best-selling author, mental health advocate, creator and host of the Pretty Gaysic podcast, and TV personality. Dean has given a TEDx talk, appeared on BuzzFeed, and directed several short films.

As a host, Dean piloted his first-ever podcast, Pretty Gaysic with Dean Lin in 2019 and has since then been in distribution through multiple platforms, including Apple Podcasts, Spotify, iHeartRadio, Google Podcasts, Stitcher, TuneIn, and more. Dean inspires his listeners by breaking traditional podcast format, talking about mental health, relationshits (relationships), and self-love.

He currently resides in Los Angeles, California. To learn more, you can visit #DeansWayOut, www.deanwlin.com, and www.prettygaysic.com.

www.ingramcontent.com/pod-product-compliance
Lightning Source LLC
Chambersburg PA
CBHW021952290426
44108CB00012B/1044